FISHER LMC

CHAPTER II

FISHER LMC

CHAPTER II

THE
BOY SCOUTS

THE BOY SCOUTS

CAROLYN SOTO

Exeter Books

NEW YORK

A Bison Book

Copyright © 1987
by Bison Books Corp

First Published in USA 1987
by Exeter Books
Distributed by Bookthrift
Exeter is a trademark of Bookthrift
Marketing, Inc.
Bookthrift is a registered trademark of
Bookthrift Marketing, Inc.
New York, New York

ALL RIGHTS RESERVED

ISBN 0-671-08914-5

Printed in Hong Kong

Edited by Timothy Jacobs and John Kirk
Designed by Ruth DeJauregui

C.1

Page 1: The old-style Boy Scout campaign hat was first adopted as head-gear by Sir Robert Baden-Powell while soldiering, and becoming 'the hero of Mafeking,' in Africa—at which time the Scouting movement was incipient (but not yet itself even an idea) in the very soldiering that 'BP' was so excellently doing.

Pages 2-3: This Canadian Scout wears a Scouting 75th Anniversary patch on his right breast pocket and a council patch identifying his national region on his right sleeve. The white diamond enclosing a red maple leaf on his left sleeve is a version of the Scouts Canada national patch, as is the patch on his wool beret, which, in bearing the international Scouting trefoil, stands for the world wide Scouting unity of which Scouts Canada is a part.

This page: These high-spirited Scouts were photographed at a national jamboree. In a mad dash around a tight turn, these boys epitomize Scouting enthusiasm, and pulling 'the Honey Wagon' as they are, they're sure to have a very enthusiastic crowd of followers, too.

CONTENTS

WORLD-WIDE SCOUTING

Boy Scouting teaches a young person to become a good citizen of whatever country he calls home. Training in responsible citizenship, physical and mental development, character guidance through group activity, patrol activity, recognition through awards and learning by doing comprise the international program of Boy Scouting. Over 16 million participants subscribe to the worldwide principles and universal practices that unite boys, young men, and adults in nearly 120 countries. Worldwide principles include: duty to God and respect for individual beliefs; loyalty to one's country and respect for its laws; strength of world friendship and Scouting brotherhood; service to others; regard for the Scout Promise and Law as a life guide; voluntary membership; independence from political influence and control; and outdoor program orientation.

Robert Stephenson Smyth Baden-Powell had the idea to train men in scouting when he was an army officer in the 5th Dragoon Guards, India. In 1899 he wrote a handbook for soldiers about survival in the field called *Aids to Scouting for N-COs and Men.* A woman named Charlotte Mason, who founded a college for training women teachers, was so impressed with Baden-Powell's book that she used it as one of her texts.

Also adopting the text, although unofficially, were numbers of young boys who were fascinated by the idea of being scouts during the South African Boer War. The boys were members of Lord Edward Cecil's Cadet Corps, who carried out responsible work for the British Army: carrying messages and supplies from the supply headquarters at Mafeking, a small town in South Africa. Robert Baden-Powell became celebrated as the 'Hero of Mafeking' after leading his 800 men against 9000 Boer soldiers who had surrounded and besieged Mafeking for 217 days. In 1900 he became the youngest Major-General in the army.

After the Boer War, Baden-Powell organized the South African Constabulary and designed a uniform for them that later became the basic Boy Scout uniform. He retired from the army in 1906.

In 1907 Baden-Powell, or 'BP' as he was called, decided to hold an experimental camp, using his military training methods, for boys from different social backgrounds. He discussed his ideas with Sir William Smith, the founder of the Boy's Brigade, and other leading youth workers and

Left: **Two Scouts peruse a uniform patch midway at a national Scouting jamboree.** *Above:* **War hero and father of Scouting Robert Stephenson Smyth Baden-Powell, aka Lord Baden-Powell —affectionately called 'BP' by his Scouting progeny.**

planned the famous camp held at Brownsea Island in Poole Harbour from 25 July to 9 August 1907. 'BP' was the scoutmaster for the camp. His assistants were G W Green, H Robson and P W Everett.

The camp was such a tremendous success that B P rewrote his army handbook, called it *Scouting for Boys,* and published it in six parts beginning in January 1908.

8

Not only did Baden-Powell write the book, he also drew all the sketches that illustrated it. By the end of 1908 the book had been translated into five other languages. The Boy Scout movement was definitely off and running.

Baden-Powell discovered a year later that girls also were eager to become Scouts. It was at a 1909 Boy Scout rally at the Crystal Palace in London that Baden-Powell saw a group of girls wearing the shirts and pants of the boys' uniforms. Instead of trousers the girls wore long blue skirts, and marched in formation behind the boys. When he asked the girls who they were, they replied, 'We're the girl scouts.' They had read *Scouting for Boys* and copied their activities on their own. Baden-Powell could see immediately that girls were determined not to be left out of the Scouting movement and decided that they should have their own organization, which he asked his sister Agnes to help organize.

In 1909 King Edward VII, who had taken a great deal of interest in the Scout movement, knighted Baden-Powell in recognition of his work with boys. It was King Edward VII who inaugurated the King's Scout badge, later changed by Queen Elizabeth to Queen's Scout badge.

In 1912 Baden-Powell married Miss Olave Soames who later became the Chief Guide of the Girl Guides. Olave and Robert Baden-Powell devoted the rest of their lives to the Scouting movements. At the world jamboree in 1920, Baden-Powell was acclaimed as Chief Scout of the World— the only person to ever hold that title.

Above: **This photo of the 1967 jamboree headquarters appears to be a veritable quilt of Scouting uniforms. The spaceframe globe** *in the foreground* **is symbolic of World-Wide Scouting.** *Right:* **Indonesian Scouts 'hamming it up.'**

Baden-Powell worked throughout his life for the promotion of world brotherhood through Boy Scouting. He believed that no better way could be found than by enrolling youth in Scouting, a movement not hindered by national boundaries.

In 1920 King George V made Baden-Powell a Baron; he became Lord Baden-Powell of Gilwell, taking his title from Gilwell Park, the international training center for Scouts located just outside London.

In his last years Baden-Powell took up residence in Africa. He died there in 1941 and was buried in Nyeri, in the shadow of Mount Kenya. His tombstone bears the simple inscription: 'Robert Baden-Powell, Chief Scout of the World, born February 22nd, 1857, died January 8th, 1941' Carved into the stone are the Scout and Guide badges and the familiar circle with the dot in the center signifying 'Gone Home.'

Today, 80 years after the original concept of Boy Scouting arose, certain acts and symbols proposed by Sir Baden-Powell are familiar all over the world:

'Be Prepared'—the motto of Boy Scouting

Scout Promise and Law—similar worldwide pledge of duty to God and country

Badge—basic trefoil design

10

Above: A Leichtenstein Scout smiles the smile of international brotherhood (*below*), which is beyond simple friendship—as each Scout endeavors to live the Golden Rule. *Right:* This three-way tug of war embodies teamwork—the tie that links us even to our friendly competitors.

Left: **Scouting is popular the world over.** *Here,* **a group of Far-Eastern Scouts enjoy an activity.** *Above:* **This cap sports a French-Canadian patch commemorating the 15th World Jamboree, postponed from Iran in 1979, to Canada in 1983.**

Scout sign—three-finger sign of personal honor
handclasp—left hand handclasp
patrol system—smaller units within the larger group
good turn—basic ideal for Boy Scouts
Overcoming barriers of language and custom, these universal Scouting practices reaffirm the relevance of scouting to world brotherhood.

Composed of six delegates from each of the member Scout associations (the Boy Scouts of America is a charter member), the World Conference is the general assembly of international Scouting. Each of the 118 member associations of the World Conference adheres to the aims and principles of World Scouting and is independent from political involvement in its respective country.

At its biennial meeting, the World Conference decides upon basic cooperative efforts and adopts a plan of mutual coordination. Since 1973 the Conference has been held in Nairobi, Copenhagen, Montreal, Birmingham, Dakar, Detroit, and Munich—each city hosting assembly delegates from far and wide of varying ages.

World Conference delegates elect a 12-member executive body called the World Scout Committee which represents the Conference between the meetings of the full Conference. Members of the Committee are elected for a term of six years with one-third retiring at each conference. The members are elected without regard to their nationality.

Supervised by the World Conference and the World Committee is the World Scout Bureau, whose general office is in Geneva, Switzerland. Regional offices administer to the African Region (office in Nairobi, Kenya), Arab Region (Cairo, Egypt), Asia-Pacific Region (Manila, Philippines), European Region (Geneva, Switzerland), and Inter-American Region (San Jose, Costa Rica).

The World Bureau is administered by the secretary-general who is supported by a small staff of technical resource personnel. The staff helps associations improve and broaden their Scouting by training professionals and volunteers. It also establishes sound financial policies and money-raising techniques, improves community facilities and procedures, and assists in marshaling the national resources of each country where Scouting is practiced. The staff also helps arrange global events such as world jamborees, encourages regional events and acts as liaison between Scouting and other international organizations. A current major effort of the World Bureau staff is to extend Boy Scouting's 'Good Turn' ideal into the emerging nations, for community development.

The Boy Scouts of America began the World Friendship Fund in the last days of World War II, when they realized

Above: A Scout from Finland bears a smile and four merit stars.
Right: African and American Scouts work together at a jamboree.

the great and urgent need to rebuild Scouting in those nations that had been racked by war. In the years since its establishment, this voluntary fund has aided every nation in the free world where scouting is practiced, sometimes aiding emerging nations that wanted Scout programs but did not yet have them.

Contributions of Scouts and their leaders given voluntarily to the World Friendship Fund are transformed into cooperative projects that help Scout associations in other countries to strengthen and extend their Scout programs. Recently completed projects include: producing Spanish-language training filmstrips for use throughout Latin America, providing camping equipment for national training centers and providing subscriptions to *Boys' Life* magazine in braille to 60 schools for the blind. Over the years American Scouts and leaders have donated more than $800,000 in World Friendship Funds to help others.

Individual businesses, corporations and foundations can support Scouting worldwide through the United States Foundation for International Scouting. The foundation has full tax privileges and is not a private foundation. Its funds are used for continued programs in Scouting for the Handicapped, community development in less-developed countries, Kandersteg International Camp in Switzerland, and professional training scholarships for overseas staff people.

World jamborees, held every four years, are among the most important events in international Scouting. Thou-

sands of Scouts from all over the world meet each other, exchange ideas and make friends. The shared ideal of world friendship overcomes barriers of language, race, custom or religion. Flags from all the nations represented fly over the jamboree whose events include demonstrations from every nation. Clothing, customs, hobbies, crafts, history and music from every part of the world are shared by Scouts at a world jamboree. Scouts compete in Scout skills, sample each other's food and, in camping together, find that their differences are small compared to their shared Scouting principles and the desire for international understanding.

The first world jamboree was held in Great Britain in 1920. Three hundred scouts from 32 countries answered Baden-Powell's invitation and camped together that first time. Every four years since then, except during World War II, scouts have met in world jamborees.

Jamborees have been held in England, Denmark, Hungary, Holland, France, Austria, Canada, the Philippines, Greece, the United States, Japan and Norway since then. England and Canada have each hosted two jamborees over the years. The largest jamboree of 50,000 Scouts and Scouters was the third World Scout Jamboree held in England in 1929. The next largest was the ninth, attended by 32,000 Scouts and Scouters, and again held in England in 1957. The ninth jamboree commemorated the 100th anniversary of Lord Baden-Powell's birth and 50 years of British Scouting.

In 1979 the fifteenth jamboree was to have been held in Iran, but was cancelled because of political unrest. The fifteenth was instead held in 1983, in Canada.

The next world jamboree, the 16th, will be held in Australia at Cataract Scout Park about 45 minutes southeast of the Sydney airport. Its theme is 'Bringing the World Together' and it will attract nearly 14,000 Scouts and Scouters from over 100 countries who will set up their colorful tents and begin an experience to be remembered for a lifetime.

Scouts who attend will be organized into provisional troops of 36 Scouts and four adult leaders in each region.

Left: **An Australian Scout greets with a smile.** *Below:* **A world jamboree registry.** *Overleaf:* **International friendship.**

They will camp within the 395-acre Australian bushland of Cataract Scout Park, on a ridge overlooking the headwaters of the Georges River. It will be a magnificent setting for the jamboree held from 30 December 1987 through 10 January 1988. The climate will surprise some of the attendees who will leave cold winter climates to enjoy Australia's summer temperatures which may range from 65 to 95 degrees F.

The Australian Scouts, the host group, will bring more surprise to their other English-speaking counterparts with some of their colorful terminology. A 'woggle' is a neckerchief slide, 'tucker' is something to eat and 'boiling a billy' means heating a pot of water in Australia.

Jamboree activities, however, will not at all be strange; they'll be just plain fun. Activities will test skills and allow Scouts from the world over to take part in competitive events, allowing the participants to enjoy their unique fellowship and to appreciate the pageantry of jamboree ceremonies.

Challenge Valley will be fun, although not necessarily 'clean' fun, as Scouts who travel thousands of miles to the Jamboree emerge from this challenge course of climbing, crawling and wading covered to their necks with mud. Luke's Skywalk will be another challenge—the most challenging part being stepping off a high platform to take a scary glide high over a deep ravine. The Scouts will be strapped into a harness attached to a steel cable—perfectly safe, but a challenge just the same. The Bike Bungle will appear to be an ordinary bicycle course until the Scouts get under way. Patrols have to first assemble the bike from assorted parts. Then one rider from the patrol pedals over the course through a water hazard and up steep hills. Just fine with the rider, but the rest of his patrol has to accompany him on foot! Teamwork is crucial to finishing the Bike Bungle. Other events are challenging in other ways—electronics and medieval games supply different diversions—but the experience of delight in activities with other international Scouts remains the reason for such international get-togethers.

The American Boy Scouts who attend the jamboree will first make application to local councils and meet qualifications for attendance similar to those met by other international Scouts. The Boy Scout from the United States must be a registered Boy Scout or Varsity Scout, at least 13 and one-half years of age, of First Class Rank and not older than 18. He'll participate in prejamboree training experience, file a health and medical record before the prejamboree training, and has to be active in a troop or team for at least six months. He'll the jamboree with the approval of his Scoutmaster or Varsity Scout coach and his local council.

The purpose of world jamborees is to provide a dramatic demonstration of Scouting's ability to develop world brotherhood, a spirit of friendship and a source of understanding among young people. Jamborees provide the opportunity for each Scout to catch the spirit and transmit it to fellow Scouts throughout the world.

Undoubtedly many lifelong pen pals will be made in Australia, and many keepsakes exchanged as in past jamborees. What is wonderful about a world jamboree is the fact that Scouts can share the same activities and sense of goodwill even though they may not share languages, customs or religions. They belong to the worldwide brotherhood of Scouting, and that apparently is enough.

SCOUTING IN THE UNITED STATES

Several dedicated men pioneered the Boy Scout program in the early years of this century. They shared a vision of a program of outdoor activities that developed skills in young boys. At the same time, such a program would provide enjoyment, fellowship and a code of conduct for everyday living. It was the type of program that, although educational, was not provided by schools.

A variety of youth groups, many using the word 'scout' in their names, were organized by men in this country and abroad. One of these men, American naturalist Ernest Thompson Seton began a group called the Woodcraft Indians. In 1902 he wrote a guidebook called *The Birch Bark Roll* for the boys in his organization.

Meanwhile, across the Atlantic in England, Robert Baden-Powell had returned from military duty in Africa as a hero. He was surprised to find young boys reading a manual he had written for his men about survival in the wild. He rewrote his manual as a nonmilitary skillbook and called it *Scouting for Boys*. The book quickly gained popularity in England and then in the United States. Troops had already begun to spring up spontaneously in the United States by the time Baden-Powell held the first Boy Scout campout on Brownsea Island off the coast of England in 1907.

About this same time Chicago publisher William D Boyce had been touring in England. Lost in London, Boyce was led out of the dense fog by an unnamed English Boy Scout who refused the tip Boyce offered for his Good Turn. The incident inspired Boyce to meet Baden-Powell, the man whose Scouting book had touched his own life. After returning to America, Boyce incorporated the Boy Scouts of America (BSA) in 1910. Immediately after its incorporation, the YMCA (Young Men's Christian Association) helped the BSA to organize a task force that would help community organizations begin and maintain a high quality Scouting program. The combined efforts resulted in the nation's first Scout camp at Lake George, NY, directed by Ernest Thompson Seton, formerly of the Woodcraft Indians. He was assisted in the camping effort by Daniel Carter Beard, who had established another youth scouting group, the Sons of Daniel Boone. Beard's group,

incidentally, later merged with the Boy Scouts of America. Also attending the historic camp was James E West, a lawyer and advocate of children's rights. West later became the first professional Chief Scout Executive of the BSA, Seaton became the first volunteer national Chief Scout and Beard became the first national Scout Commissioner. From differing perspectives but with similar goals, the efforts of all these pioneering men came together in the Boy Scouts of America.

Incorporated on 8 February 1910, the Boy Scouts of America was chartered by Congress in 1916. Its purpose then, as now, was to provide an educational program for boys and young adults to build character, to train in the responsibilities of participating citizenship, and to develop personal fitness. Many community groups which have goals compatible with those of the Boy Scouts of America have received national charters to use the Scouting program in their own youth work. Such groups include educational, religious, civic, fraternal, business, labor, governmental bodies, corporations, professional associations and citizens. Each chartered organization provides a meeting place and adult volunteer leadership for its Boy Scouts.

The Boy Scouts of America (BSA) program provides activities and training suitable for boys of different age groups, encompassing ages seven to twenty—from Tiger Cubs to Explorer Scouts. More than 70 million individuals have held membership in the BSA since 1910. Included in that membership are some of the country's most distinguished men, not the least of whom is former president Gerald Ford. Currently, nearly five million individuals hold membership in the BSA.

Youth members of the BSA contribute to Boy Scouting through nominal membership dues. Each Scout buys his own uniform, handbook and personal equipment and pays his own camp fees. Membership dues help individual packs, troops, teams and posts to meet their expenses for their activities and supplies.

Coordinating the administrative activity of packs, troops, teams and posts are local councils which provide professional staff supervision. Local councils train volunteer leaders and maintain council camps. They provide council service centers where volunteer leaders can obtain literature, insignia, advancement badges, and other items

Left: **This very attentive Boy Scouts of America contingent was photographed while attending the 15th World Jamboree.**

vital to Boy Scouting. Each council maintains records that account for its activity and membership. More than 400 local councils and six regional service centers meet the needs of their youth.

Although each council is financially autonomous, the national organization of the Boy Scouts of America provides services and coordinates a communications network nationwide through its magazines and literature. Program development, camp and office planning, financial counseling, and professional personnel are available through the national organization. National events such as jamborees, Explorer Presidents' Association Congress, National Eagle Scout Association conferences, Order of the Arrow conferences, and National Council are administered by the national office.

In all its activities the national office aims to create a climate of positive understanding and support for the Scouts and leaders who are a part of the BSA. Likewise the Scouts and leaders contribute to the national organization through their registration fees, subscriptions to *Scouting* and *Boys' Life* magazines and purchase of uni-

Below: **At world jamborees, Scouts learn to appreciate one another's often very different cultural values, as seen in this photo of Irish Scouts.** *Right:* **This Scout demonstrates typical Scout economy—as he empties the rinsewater, he cleans the bench for later use.**

forms and equipment. The national organization also is supported by contributions from individuals and foundation grants that help to deliver the Boy Scouts of America program to each of its chartered organizations. The national organization maintains liaison with 118 Scouting associations in other countries, as a member of the World Scout Conference.

Character development, citizenship training and personal fitness are the three specific objectives of the Scouting program. They are commonly referred to as the 'Aims of Scouting,' and manifest themselves in the Scout motto, 'Be Prepared,' and the Scout slogan, 'Do a Good Turn Daily.' Boy Scouts pledge themselves to the Scout Oath, also called the Scout Promise:

On my honor I will do my best
To do my duty to God and my country and to obey the Scout Law;
To help other people at all times;
To keep myself physically strong, mentally awake, and morally straight.

The Scout Law defines the characteristics of a Boy Scout:

Trustworthy—A Scout tells the truth. He keeps his promises. Honesty is part of his code of conduct. People can depend on him.

Loyal—A Scout is true to his family, Scout leaders, friends, school and nation.

Helpful—A Scout is concerned about other people. He does things willingly for others without pay or reward.

Friendly—A Scout is a friend to all. He is a brother to other Scouts. He seeks to understand others. He respects those with ideas and customs other than his own.

Courteous—A Scout is polite to everyone regardless of age or position. He knows good manners make it easier for people to get along together.

Kind—A Scout understands there is strength in being gentle. He treats others as he wants to be treated. He does not hurt or kill harmless things without reason.

Obedient—A Scout follows the rules of his family, school and troop. He obeys the laws of his community and country. If he thinks these rules and laws are unfair, he tries to have them changed in an orderly manner rather than disobey them.

Cheerful—A Scout looks for the bright side of things. He cheerfully does the tasks that come his way. He tries to make others happy.

Thrifty—A Scout works to pay his way and to help others. He saves for unforseen needs. He protects and conserves natural resources. He carefully uses time and property.

Brave—A Scout can face danger even if he is afraid. He has the courage to stand for what he thinks is right even if others laugh at or threaten him.

Clean—A Scout keeps his body and mind fit and clean. He goes around with those who believe in living by these same ideals. He helps keep his home and community clean.

Reverent—A Scout is reverent toward God. He is faithful in his religious duties. He respects the beliefs of others.

The Scout Oath, the Scout Law, the Scout motto and the Scout slogan allow a Boy Scout to measure himself by the ideals they contain and encourage his striving to reach the goals.

CUB SCOUTS

Cub Scouting began in 1930 when the Boy Scouts of America created an opportunity for younger boys to enjoy the Scouting experience. Cub Scouting emphasizes involvement between Scouts and their parents, and of course encourages friendships among the boys. Any boy in the second through fifth grades (or age 8, 9 or 10) may become a Cub Scout by joining a pack. He is assigned to a den composed usually of boys who form a natural play group. Theirs are year-round, home-centered programs used by chartered organizations such as schools or churches. Dens meet weekly and are supervised by a volunteer den leader, usually the mother or father of one of the boys (a 'den mother' or 'den leader'). An assistant den leader and a den chief (an older Scout) may also help the den leader with activities. One of the Cub Scouts is elected by the Scouts in his den to be the 'denner' who assists the den leader and den chief.

All the dens in a neighborhood come together monthly for a pack meeting under the direction of a Cubmaster and pack committee. Similar packs are formed from within chartered organizations such as religious or educational bodies. The pack committee may include parents of the boys or members of the chartered organization.

At left: **These Cub Scouts seem to be having an inordinate amount of fun with their project.** *Above:* **These Scouts are shown practicing knots at the 1974 Scout-O-Rama on Okinawa.**

The Cub Scout program intends to develop habits and attitudes of good citizenship and to influence a boy's character development and spiritual growth. Its motto, 'Do Your Best,' fosters a sense of personal achievement for each boy and improves understanding within his family. Cub Scouting encourages good sportsmanship and pride in growing strong both in mind and body. It shows a boy how to be helpful and prepares him to be a Boy Scout, and all the while provides fun and exciting new things to do.

Cub Scouting is where the Boy Scout experience in the United States begins, even though a boy or young man can join Scouting at any Scout level. More boys are Cub Scouts than Boy Scouts or Explorer Scouts, the other two membership divisions of the Boy Scouts of America. As of the end of 1985, over one and a half million boys belonged to Cub Scouts (including Tiger Cubs who are first-grade boys) and formed over 51,000 packs.

Each member makes the Cub Scout Promise:
I, (the boy's name), promise to do my best
To do my duty to God and my country,
To help other people, and
To obey the Law of the Pack.

Each Cub Scout adheres to the Law of the Pack:
  The Cub Scout follows Akela (his leader).
  The Cub Scout helps the pack go.
  The pack helps the Cub Scout grow.
  The Cub Scout gives goodwill.

In expressing the basic concepts of the above oaths, Cub Scouts learn from their earliest encounter that although Scouting's ideals are high, they are attainable because they are so basic. The Cub Scout colors, blue and gold—blue for sky, truth, spirituality and loyalty; gold for warm sunlight, good cheer and happiness—symbolize the spirit of Cub Scouting.

A Tiger Cub team consists of one first-grade boy and his adult partner. Each team meets at home weekly to conduct activities that involve the whole family. The team meets with four to eight other teams monthly for a 'Big Idea' activity. Tiger Cubs have their own program but are affiliated with a Cub Scout pack which once or twice a year invites the Tiger Cubs for special activities.

At the end of his first-grade year, a Tiger Cub graduates into the affiliated pack to become a Cub Scout. He has completed the first step in a plan of advancement that emphasizes learning by doing.

To be a Bobcat, a boy has learned the Cub Scout promise, Law of the Pack, handshake, salute, sign and motto with the help of his parents. He may then begin on his Wolf achievements.

The twelve achievements are: Feats of Skill, Your Flag, Keep your Body Healthy, Know Your Home and Community, Tools for Fixing and Building, Start a Collection, Your Living World, Cooking and Eating, Be Safe at Home and on the Street, Family Fun, Duty to God and Making Choices. When the Cub Scout has completed the achievements, the Wolf badge is his award. He may then continue to work on other Wolf electives in 22 different areas. He receives a Gold Arrow Point when he has completed 10 projects in the elective areas. For each additional 10 projects he receives a Silver Arrow Point.

A Cub Scout in the second grade, or nine years old, begins working on 24 Bear achievements divided into four groups: God, Country, Family and Self. Of the 24 achievements, a Cub Scout must earn 12—one from the first group, three from the second, four from the third and four from the fourth. The achievements are: Ways We Worship; Emblems of Faith; What Makes America Special?; Tall Tales; Sharing Your World with Wildlife; Take Care of Your Planet; Law Enforcement Is a Big Job!; The Past Is Exciting and Important; What's Cooking?; Family Fun; Be Ready!; Family Outdoor Adventures; Saving Well, Spending Well; Ride Right; Games-Games-Games!; Building Muscles; Information, Please; Jot It Down; Shavings and

Cub Scout dens are active and the boys like having fun. Helping to renew our resources, these Cubs (*below*) gather at a recycling center, while another Cub den (*at right*) has fun creating a scarecrow—which might be part of a Bear Adventure.

Chips; Sawdust and Nails; Build a Model; Typing It All Up; Sports, Sports, Sports; and Be a Leader. Once he achieves the Bear badge, a Cub Scout may work on Bear electives (and earning Gold and Silver Arrow Points) until he becomes a Webelos Scout.

'Webelos' is the code name for 'We'll be loyal Scouts' and is pronounced Wee-buh-lohs. A Cub Scout graduates into a Webelos den when he is ten years old, and at this point is called a Webelos Scout rather than Cub Scout. He wears a different uniform that displays his new status. He attends meetings in the early evening or on Saturday. He takes part in a program more challenging than before and is led by a den chief who is more experienced. His advancement record, previously kept by his parent, is now recorded by his Webelos den leader and the Webelos Scout begins work immediately on the Webelos badge. Cub Scouting's highest honor, the Arrow of Light Award, becomes attainable to a Scout who earns a Webelos badge. Working towards the Webelos badge, a Webelos Scout can earn 15 activity badges: Aquanaut, Artist, Athlete, Citizen, Craftsman, Engineer, Forester, Geologist, Naturalist, Outdoorsman, Scholar, Scientist, Showman, Sportsman and Traveler. When he's reached age 11 (or age 10 and a half and completed the fifth grade), the Webelos Scout is ready to join a Boy Scout troop.

Cub Scouts begin an activity at their weekly den meetings. During the week the Scout finishes the project with his parents' help, and one of his parents signs his Cub

Above: **A Cub Scout from an Air Force den paints a P-51 Mustang scale model.** *Right:* **Boy Scouts of America encompasses many ethnic backgrounds. These sober Arizona Cubs are learning first aid.** *Overleaf:* **Besides the abundance of US flags in evidence at this international jamboree are the flags of many other countries, and assorted troop banners.**

Scout book if the project is one required for Wolf or Bear advancement. Parents are in this way involved in Scout activity which strengthens family ties. Cub Scouts and their families attend pack meetings together, allowing parents to see their sons involved as Scouts. The first portion of pack meetings is spent informally, possibly viewing exhibits or in group-gathering activity. The second portion of the meeting is more structured, opening formally and following a program of activity such as skits or songs related to a monthly theme. Awarding of badges might be a part of a pack meeting.

Cub Scouts are encouraged in outdoor adventure programs. These programs might include den field trips, picnics and outings. Day camps are conducted by nearly all Scouting councils. Family camping (even in the backyard) is emphasized for younger Cub Scouts, and overnight or extended camping experiences are provided for Webelos Scouts through their councils.

Team sports are favorites of Cub Scouts who are encouraged to be physically fit. Sports or other competitive events occur at the pack or interpack levels. The Cub Scout sports program offers up to 18 different sports.

BOY SCOUTS

Boy Scouting is open to boys who are at least 10 and one-half years old and have completed the fifth grade or who are 11 through 17 years old. The three 'Aims of Scouting' are met by focusing on a vigorous program of outdoor activities. Boy Scouting, like other phases of the Scouting program, is made available to community organizations that have similar interests and goals. These organizations include professional organizations, government bodies, and religious, education, civic, fraternal, business, labor and citizens' groups and are called chartered organizations. Each chartered organization provides leadership, a meeting place and support for troop activities. One member of each organization is appointed by its members to be the Scouting coordinator.

Boy Scouts are encouraged to earn money for their Scout expenses and contribute weekly dues to their troop for budgeted items. Troops generate additional income by working on approved money-earning projects. At the community level, contributions from the United Way, sustaining membership enrollment, bequests and special contributions support Boy Scouting. These contributions provide leadership training, outdoor programs, council service centers, other facilities and professional service staff for the council.

A Boy Scout plans his advancement and progresses at his own pace as he overcomes each challenge offered. To advance in Boy Scouts, a boy must be loyal to the ideals of Scouting and must pass various tests of skill and knowledge. Whenever a Scout is ready to advance from one rank to another, he has a personal conference with his Scoutmaster. During such a conference the Scout and the leader review the Scout's progress and discuss what course he should follow for advancement. Rewarded for each achievement, the Boy Scout gains self-confidence to attain other goals.

Scouts operate in patrols—small groups of five to eight boys. The patrol method gives Boy Scouts experience in group living and participating citizenship. One Boy Scout is elected the leader of his patrol, but all members of the

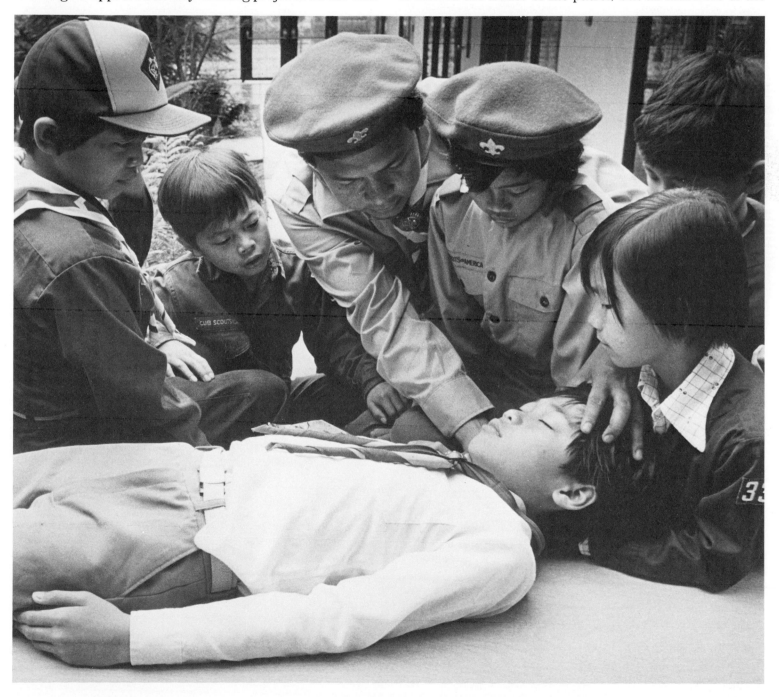

patrol share some responsibility for the patrol activities. Usually four patrols make up a troop, and they are led by an adult Scoutmaster who may be assisted by other adults.

After participating in troop and patrol activities for at least two months, a Boy Scout achieves the rank of Tenderfoot. At this first rank, the Scout knows the Scout Oath and Scout Law by heart and shows that he follows them. He is able to explain the meaning of each point of the Boy Scout Law in his own words. A Tenderfoot has already earned the Citizenship skill award and one other skill award. The awards are in activities that develop skills necessary for day-to-day living—camping, communications, community living, environment, family living, first aid, physical fitness and swimming.

For the rank of Second Class Scout, a Scout must have been an active Tenderfoot for at least two months. Further, he has earned the hiking and first aid skill awards and one other skill award.

After a Scout has been an active Second Class Scout for at least two months he becomes a First Class Scout, if he has earned the camping and cooking skill awards and one other skill award. Beyond these awards, he has passed the swimming test and has earned the first aid merit badge.

After serving as a First Class Scout for at least four months and having earned six merit badges (including four badges required for Eagle Scout), a Scout becomes a Star Scout.

A Life Scout has been a Star Scout for at least six months and has earned a total of eleven merit badges (including seven required for Eagle Scout ranking).

To become an Eagle Scout, the highest rank in Scouting, a boy has been a Life Scout for at least six months. He has earned eleven required merit badges and ten other merit badges. At the three highest levels of scouting (Star Scout, Life Scout and Eagle Scout), the Scout must also meet various character, service and leadership requirements.

When a Scout has attained Eagle Scout rank, he deserves much credit in having achieved Scouting's highest award. His character is tested by the Eagle Scout Challenge to wear his award with humility, keeping in mind that the Eagle Scout is looked up to as an example. The Challenge is addressed to the Eagle Scout, reiterating the responsibilities that come with the award.

The first responsibility is to live with honor. It is the reason that the very first point of the Scout Law is 'A Scout is trustworthy.' By living honorably, an Eagle Scout shows not only that honor is important to him, but that he also understands that he sets an example for other Scouts. In living honorably he brings credit to his home, his church, his troop and his community. The white part of the tri-colored ribbon on his Eagle Scout badge represents honor.

Below: **Boy Scouts donate used clothing to an orphanage.** *Right:* **San Francisco Scouts sit astride a scooter.**

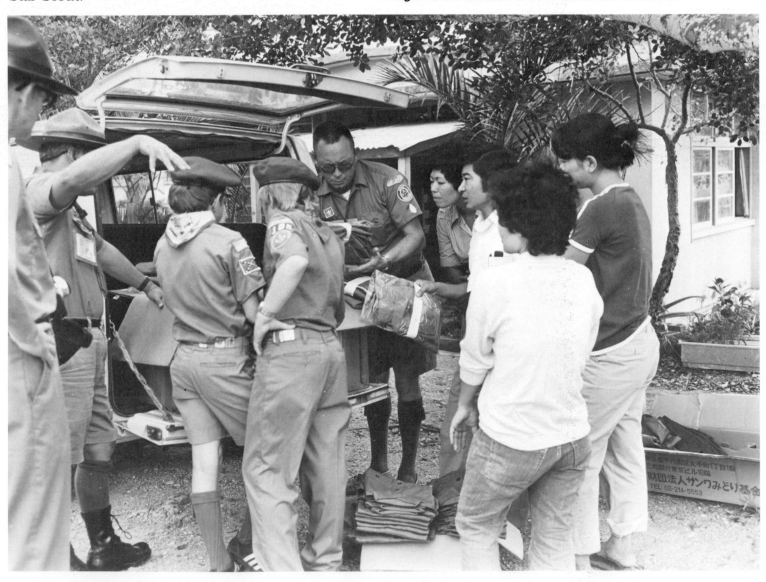

The second obligation of an Eagle Scout is loyalty. His loyalty to his troop and brother Scouts makes him 'pitch in' and carry his share of the load. Loyalty means devotion to community, to country, to personal ideals and to God. The blue part of the ribbon reminds the Eagle Scout to remain loyal.

The third obligation of an Eagle Scout is courage. It is a measure by which men measure themselves and others. An Eagle Scout knows that courage means not only bravery in the face of physical danger, but also the determination to stand up for the right. An Eagle Scout seeks his share of the world's work, and the red part of the Eagle Scout badge reminds him to be courageous in his life.

The fourth obligation of an Eagle Scout is to be cheerful. To remind him of this responsibility, the red, white and blue ribbon of his badge is attached to the scroll of the Second Class Scout award, which has its ends turned up in a smile.

The final responsibility of an Eagle Scout is service. The Eagle Scout extends help to Scouts who are not yet Eagles, in the same way that others helped him to reach his rank. The performance of a daily Good Turn takes on a new meaning as his adult life continues to demonstrate service to others. The Eagle protects the weak and helpless. He aids and comforts the unfortunate and the oppressed. He upholds the rights of others while defending his own. He will always 'Be Prepared' to put forth his best.

The Eagle Scout is challenged to allow the Scout Oath and the Scout Law to guide him for the rest of his life.

Eagle Scout Palms are awarded to Eagle Scouts who have earned more than the 21 required badges. A Bronze Palm is awarded for five additional merit badges, a Gold Palm for 10 and a Silver Palm for 15. Scouts may earn awards for distinguished service with local conservation authorities, for service to their church, for special camping ability and for passing the requirements for Scout Life Guard. The National Court of Honor awards certificates of heroism or Honor Medals, given to a Scout who has saved the life of another person at the risk of his own life.

Below and right: **The 'Twin Cities' police department of Larkspur and Corte Madera, California sponsors an Explorer troop. Members of both sexes can be Explorers.** *Overleaf:* **Explorer Scouts, and the Explorer spacecraft, circa 1958.**

EXPLORERS

Young adults from ages 15 through 20 may be Explorers. Explorers share interest and experience in areas that include careers, citizenship, fitness, social events, service projects and outdoor activities. Explorer posts—organized by businesses, industries, religious groups, government agencies, professional societies, civic clubs, labor unions and other community organizations—have programs that match the interest of the young adults in the posts. A program in data processing, for example, might be designed by a computer center for its Explorer post. Likewise, an aeronautical firm might design a program for Explorers who have an interest in aviation. Each Explorer post concentrates its activities on a particular vocation or interest.

Many corporations encourage their local branches to organize Explorer posts providing opportunities for young men and women to learn about careers and free enterprise. Some of these corporations have more than 20 posts. They include Alcoa, Burlington Northern, General Motors, IBM, Kodak, McDonnell Douglas, Sears Roebuck, US Steel and others.

The program of each post is developed around the interests and capabilities of the adults in the organization, but all share the purpose of Exploring—the improvement of character, citizenship and fitness.

Career programs feature the understanding of America's society, economy, and government through hands-on career experiences. Some school districts have organized in-school programs called Career Awareness Exploring that are supported by local BSA councils. Career Awareness Exploring provides a series of career seminars for students. Citizenship activities prepare Explorers for leadership, civic participation and pride of heritage. Fitness and sports programs promote physical and emotional well-being. Social events develop social skills and encourage the growth of personal and religious values. Service projects encourage respect for others and the desire to help others. Outdoor activities teach self reliance and appreciation for the environment.

Almost every Explorer post specializes in a specific career, hobby, sport or outdoor program area. But some of the more than 100 specialties are so popular that they have their own national committees, activities and staff support. Among them are:

Aviation—This specialty comprises a wide range of programs including maintenance, gliders, operations, construction, flight attendants, airport management and aerospace. The Aircraft Owners and Pilots Association Air Safety Foundation and other aviation organizations, unions and industries has supported this popular program.

Law and Government—Supported by the American Bar Association and other associations, this specialty provides Explorers with first-hand experience in America's legal and court system through Law Day activities, mock trials and other law-related activities.

Law Enforcement—A grant from the Law Enforcement Assistance Administration, endorsement by the International Association of Chiefs of Police and help from other national law enforcement organizations and industries support this Explorer specialty. More than 1700 police

and sheriff's departments have organized posts specializing in law enforcement.

Medical and Health Careers—National health organizations such as the American Medical Association support the organization of posts in hospitals, clinics, medical centers, schools and other health-care organizations. These posts serve Explorers by providing insight into a variety of career opportunities and serve their communities at the same time.

Outdoor Adventure—Camping, hiking, canoeing, ecology, mountaineering, field sports and fishing are some of the outdoor activities in this specialty that stresses conservation, safety and proper outdoor living.

Sea Exploring—The oldest specialty program started as Sea Scouts in 1912 and has grown to include oceanography, sailing and power boating. Explorers learn traditional seamanship, modern nautical techniques and ocean safety in this popular maritime specialty.

Sports—Explorers can develop their sports talents in this specialty whose sponsors include the US Olympic Committee. Some posts specialize in one sport while others offer a variety of sports and fitness programs. Explorers can enjoy competition and also learn coaching, training, officiating, nutrition and career building.

Over one million people belong to 27,000 Explorer posts. The membership figures include 630,000 Career Awareness Explorers and 94,000 adults. The 392,000 Explorers include young women and men from throughout the United States who appreciate the fun, challenge, excitement and worth of the Explorer program.

A variety of awards and scholarships is available to recognize achievements of Explorers.

Members receive a subscription to *Exploring*, a quarterly journal that influences and enriches their lives as it highlights the excitement of Exploring.

VARSITY SCOUTS

Varsity Scouting is the Boy Scouts of America's exciting, fun-filled and challenging program for mid-teenaged boys. It is designed to positively influence a young man's character and his physical, mental, social and cultural development. Varsity Scouting is not a sports program although it can involve sports. It is called 'varsity' because it is the senior team of Boy Scouting. The program was begun in 1978 as an experiment in 28 scout-

Left: **The Larkspur-Corte Madera, California Explorer troop.**
Above: **These turn of the century Sea Scouts practice their seamanship on the San Francisco Bay.**

ing councils around the country. It was introduced nationwide in 1984.

Boys who are 14 (or graduates of the eighth grade) to 17 years old may join Varsity Scouting, although the chartered organizations using the Varsity program may determine actual limits within this age range. These chartered organizations provide membership, leadership personnel, administration and meeting facilities and the Boy Scouts of America provides the program-related materials and organization.

Rather than traditional troops, Varsity Scouts belong to teams. Their adult leader is called a Coach instead of a Scoutmaster. Their youth leader is a team captain instead of a senior patrol leader. The team may be divided into squads.

Varsity Scouting comprises five program fields of emphasis. Each Varsity Scout is expected to take part in all five—Advancement, High-Adventure Activities, Personal Development, Service and Special Programs and Events.

Advancement—Scouting's highest advancement honor, Eagle Scout rank, is achievable in Varsity Scouting.

Varsity Scouts follow the same requirements as Boy Scouts. Special recognitions in Scouting such as the 50-Miler Award and Mile Swim are also earned by Varsity Scouts.

High-Adventure Activities—These activities beyond the reach of younger Scouts emphasize the application of skills already learned. Opportunities for personal challenges are available at one of the Boy Scouts of America's high-adventure bases, on historic trails, through international travel or in other noncamping activities.

Personal Development—Growth through spirituality, leadership abilities, citizenship, social and cultural attributes and physical fitness are promoted through Varsity Scouting.

Service—Emphasized until it becomes a constant ingredient of daily experience, service is practiced by each Varsity Scout and each Varsity Scout team through projects which they conceive, manage and carry out.

Special Programs and Events—Here is the chance for competitive team and individual sports, special programs and events at all local to national levels.

When a Varsity Scout has completed specific requirements in each of the five program fields of emphasis, he

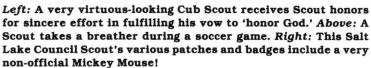

Left: **A very virtuous-looking Cub Scout receives Scout honors for sincere effort in fulfilling his vow to 'honor God.'** *Above:* **A Scout takes a breather during a soccer game.** *Right:* **This Salt Lake Council Scout's various patches and badges include a very non-official Mickey Mouse!**

earns the 'VS' (Varsity Scout) letter for his Varsity jacket. Bars sewn beneath the 'VS' mean that the Scout has qualified for additional letters.

The Varsity Scout jacket can be worn with either of the Varsity Scout uniforms—the official field uniform of the Boy Scouts of America with distinctive blaze-color shoulder loops or the Varsity Scout T-shirt and brown trousers.

Each Varsity Scout agrees to accept and live by the Varsity Scout pledge:

As a Varsity Scout I will: live by the Scout Oath, Law, motto, and slogan; honor the dignity and worth of all persons; promote the cause of freedom; and do my best to be a good team member.

LONE SCOUTS

Along with Scout organizations in Canada, New Zealand, Malta, Gibralter, South Africa and Burma, the Boy Scouts of America is concerned with serving boys (in isolated areas or) unable to join a Scouting unit. Such a boy can become a member as a Lone Cub Scout or Lone Boy Scout.

Any boy eligible to join a Scout troop or pack might find himself in a situation that prevents his joining. A boy in this situation might be the son of parents who work overseas or are in the military, an exchange student, severely handicapped, living in a rural area or a migrant worker.

A boy registers as a Lone Scout through a local Scouting council. The only exception to this practice is an American boy who resides in a country without a Scouting program; in this case he registers directly with the National council.

Each Lone Scout must have an adult US citizen who agrees to serve as his counselor. The adult may be a male parent, guardian, minister, teacher or adult friend. A female adult may serve as counselor to a Lone Cub Scout. The counselor encourages, instructs, examines and reviews the boy at steps toward advancement in Scouting.

A Lone Scout may advance just the same as a Cub Scout or Boy Scout who belongs to a pack or troop. His activities may tend towards independent action and self-reliance activities or units of special skills suitable to his situation, but he is encouraged to communicate (by letter, radio, writing for special publications, etc) with other Lone Scouts.

Lone Scouts are encouraged to wear a uniform the same as other Scouts, which can help give the boy a feeling of belonging and support. Lone Scouts may wear the Lone Scout Medallion on the left sleeve and a Lone Scout neckerchief. They can also wear any of the other Cub Scout or Boy Scout badges and insignia. Over 200 boys presently are active Lone Scouts.

What may sound like a lonely Scouting experience has nevertheless been the experience of hundreds of thousands of former Lone Scouts who found it rewarding and enriching. Many former Lone Scouts have become active adult members of Boy Scouts, showing their support of the Scouting experience by giving of their time and money.

SCOUTING FOR THE HANDICAPPED

Ever since its founding, the Boy Scouts of America has had fully participating members who suffered from physical, mental and emotional disabilities. In fact the first Chief Scout Executive, Dr James E West was handicapped. The BSA has directed itself to keep handicapped boys in the mainstream of Scouting, but it has also recognized the special needs of those with severe handicaps.

In 1923 a special badge was created for Scouts whose permanent physical disabilities prevented them from passing all the requirements for Second and First Class Scout. *The Official Boy Scout Handbook* has had Braille editions for many years, and merit badge pamphlets have been recorded on cassette tapes for blind Scouts. In 1965 over-age mentally retarded persons became eligible to register as Scouts, and today that privilege is extended to all severely handicapped persons. In 1975 the National Executive Committee removed all age restrictions on advancement of severely handicapped Scouts, thereby allowing Cub Scouts over 11, Boy Scouts over 18 and Explorers over 21 to continue to advance at their own pace for as long as they remain members of the Boy Scouts of America.

A grant from the Disabled American Veterans in 1970 enabled the BSA to establish a Handicapped Service in its Relationships Division. In 1974 the National Advisory Committee on Scouting for the Handicapped (NACOSH) was formed. Nearly 63,000 handicapped persons are involved in Scouting's special unit programs in about 4000 community organizations. An additional estimated 100,000 to 150,000 handicapped Scouts and Explorers are registered in regular Scouting units.

Much of the work of the program on Scouting for the handicapped is directed at helping unit leaders develop an awareness of the handicapped persons. Troop leaders are encouraged to include handicapped Scouts in regular Cub Scout packs, Boy Scout troops, Varsity Scout teams or Explorer posts. In that way, Scouting offers youth with handicaps a chance to be like other youth their age.

Many special Scouting units are located in special schools or centers that charter Scouting programs. Many Scouting units, therefore, are composed of members with identical handicaps. The entire troop may be blind, deaf or share a handicap that requires wheelchairs. Members of these handicapped troops are nonetheless encouraged to participate in Scouting activities at the district, council, area, regional and national levels where they can enjoy Scouting alongside Scouts without handicaps in the brotherhood of Scouting.

Almost one-third of the local Scouting councils have established their own advisory committees on Scouting for the handicapped patterned after NACOSH. These committees develop and coordinate effective Scouting programs for handicapped Scouts, using all available

Below and right: **The true strength of a Scout is most often measured in terms of character, brotherly love and courage.**

"We don't know you, but we love you."
—Troop 555

Imagine what it's like to be a blind kid learning to pitch a tent. Imagine being born with your heart outside your chest cavity and still achieving the rank of Eagle Scout. Most of the Scouts in Troop 555 have physical or mental disabilities. But thanks to your United Way contributions, they're busy beating the odds.

United Way of the Bay Area

The San Francisco Bay Area Council Boy Scouts. One of the United Way agencies you support.

community resources. All local councils are encouraged to make summer and long-term camp experiences accessible to handicapped Scouts by removing physical barriers to their campsites.

Cub Scouts, Boy Scouts, Varsity Scouts and Explorers with handicaps participate in exactly the same program as their corresponding nonhandicapped peers. They must meet the same requirements as the others in all cases except one. That one exception is for moderately mentally retarded Boy Scouts. Their special advancement track and a series of badges takes them to an award equivalent to First Class Scout. If they then want to advance further, they must meet all the requirements that other Scouts meet.

Although the Boy Scouts of America's policy has always been to treat members with handicaps as much like other members as possible, some accommodations in advancement requirements have become a tradition. A Scout with a permanent physical or mental disability may select an alternate merit badge in lieu of a required badge if his handicapping condition prohibits him from completing the necessary requirements for a required merit badge as long as the substitute badge provides a 'similar learning experience.' His local council advancement committee must approve the application.

The BSA policy is designed to keep handicapped Scouts in the mainstream of Scouting as much as possible. Leaders receive suggestions for practical policy applications in approach and methods. A Scout in a wheelchair can meet

The Boy Scouts honor God by truly engaging their often-diverse faiths. These Scouts met Pope Paul VI (*below*). *Right:* Two Scouts contemplate Brother Barnabas, founder of Lincoln Hall Catholic High School in Lincolndale, NY.

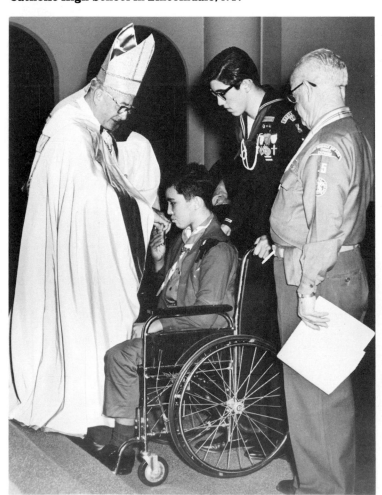

Above: A Scout 'holds the log down' as others man the crosscut saw.

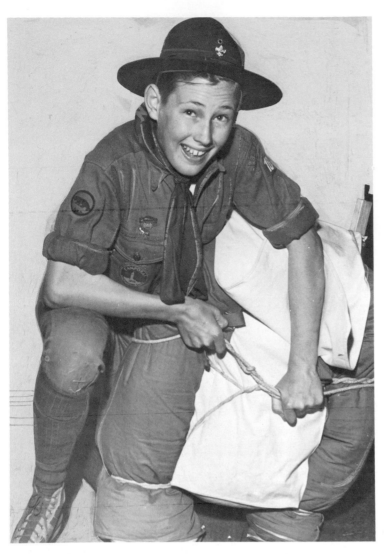

Above and right: **The Scout uniform of the '30s and '40s is gone, but the 'ready to go!' Scout eagerness is timeless.**

the hiking requirement by taking a trip to places of interest in his community. He can meet the camping requirement by transporting his pack on his wheelchair. Obviously, a handicapped Scout's leader is crucial to the his advancement. Allowing more time or permitting the use of special aids are ways that leaders can help handicapped Scouts in their efforts to advance. Several official Boy Scout publications such as *Understanding Scouts with Handicaps, Understanding Cub Scouts with Handicaps* and *Exploring for the Handicapped* help leaders of handicapped Scouts to be as understanding as possible of physical disabilities. A resource manual, *Scouting for the Handicapped,* was first published in 1980, and the Handicap Awareness Newsletter appeared in 1983. Filmstrips on Scouting for physically handicapped youth and mentally retarded youth have been produced for use in volunteer training.

Local councils have continued to hold handicaporees and jamborettes that feature camping and outdoor activities for handicapped Scouts. They have also pioneered their own handicapped awareness trails.

The Boy Scouts of America has designed ways to bring the problems of the handicapped to the attention of nonhandicapped Scouts. At the 1977 national jamboree, the first Handicapped Awareness Trail was incorporated into the program. Many local councils have since then created their own awareness trails, designed to make nonhandicapped persons aware of the many problems

faced by the handicapped. An interpreter's strip for signing for the deaf can be earned by all Scouts as well as a handicapped awareness merit badge. The purpose of the handicapped awareness merit badge is the development of a positive attitude toward handicapped individuals. Based not just on study but also on personal involvement, both the handicapped and nonhandicapped benefit from their interaction. For the handicapped, the interaction means an excellent foundation for acceptance, mainstreaming and normalization throughout the school years and into adult life. For the nonhandicapped, the benefits extend as their new awareness is shared with other friends.

THE OFFICIAL BOY SCOUT HANDBOOK

This 576-page publication from the Boy Scouts of America is now in its ninth edition. Since its first production in 1910, nearly 32 million copies of this indispensable book have been printed. The first *Official Handbook* of the Boy Scouts of America was published hurriedly as an Americanized version of Baden-Powell's *Scouting for Boys,* published in England in 1908.

Early editions of *The Official Boy Scout Handbook* have become collector's items worth far more than their original cover prices, but any edition of the book that wears its worn, dog-eared appearance is testament to the worth placed upon it by its user.

The Handbook explains what Scouting is all about: how to become one, what it means to be a Scout, what the badges and insignia signify, what it takes to advance, etc. The Handbook points out that it is easy to *become* a Scout, but it is not easy to *be* one even though the book explains clearly what is expected of a Scout. It explains the meaning of the Scout Oath or Promise and compares itself to the Athenian Oath—sworn by 17-year-old young men in the city of Athens in ancient Greece, pledging similar goals and ideals.

In the Handbook, a Scout finds practical suggestions for his daily Good Turn and explains why it is important, and how experience as a Scout expands the opportunities to help. The Outdoor Code and outdoor safety rules are explained in the Handbook, which is illustrated with line drawings.

Practical aspects of Scout activities explained in the handbook—such as tying rope into knots, camp cookery, identifying edible wild plants, mapping, finding directions without a compass and backpacking—are the basis for lifelong learning and enjoyment of the outdoors. Handbook checklists of equipment necessary for camping, criteria for a campsite, and many drawings of equipment and explanations of their proper use would serve any camper, Scout or not.

When a Scout follows the illustrations and explanations of how to swim, lifesaving and first aid for all types of injury, he is readying himself to 'Be Prepared.' It is the kind of knowledge that is not used daily, but can actually save lives when it is needed.

The *Official Boy Scout Handbook* also teaches Scouts how to be good citizens, to know the traditions of the nation and their origins and how to prepare to be great men by first being great boys. The Handbook takes the reader on a 'hike' through the nation—describing the different geographical areas of the country. The Handbook lists some rights held by citizens and faces that list with duties that those rights call forth. It presents the proper flag ceremony and the reasons for treating the flag with respect.

The Handbook citizenship section also stresses that citizenship is important in the community and in the home, that the family is its own organization deserving all the respect Scouts promise to the larger community, that many configurations can make up a family and that whether or not the people within the family are related by blood, each member of the family cares about the others.

The many steps on the road to Eagle Scout are explained in the Scout Handbook, one of the most complete reference works in print. It tells how to advance, the requirements for attaining each rank, how the Scoutmaster can help determine the Scout's route and the evaluation of his progress in Scoutmaster conferences. The Handbook shows what the merit badges look like and tells where to find out how to earn them. This section of the Handbook speaks of setting goals, determining how they will be sought and attaining those goals.

Living the Scout Oath in growth from boyhood into manhood is explained in the Handbook. Each element of the Scout Oath is paraphrased and expanded upon, illustrating that the qualities promised in the Oath are the same qualities that make men great.

The Official Boy Scout Handbook tells a Scout just about everything he needs to know and, to help him find where it is in the book, it is fully indexed. A Scout uses his Handbook also as a record of his Scout history, with documents of his achievements ready for his adult leader's signature. A Scout can continue his trail to Eagle using the same edition of the Handbook that he began with, whether or not any changes in the requirements have been made.

This is a remarkable book, and the amount of material it contains is astounding. It should come as no surprise that *The Official Boy Scout Handbook* has outsold every other book in the United States except *The Bible*.

ORDER OF THE ARROW

The Order of the Arrow (OA) was founded by Dr E Urner Goodman and Carroll A Edson in 1915 at the Philadelphia Council's Treasure Island Camp. It was an experimental program until 1934 when the Order of the Arrow was approved as part of the Scouting program. In 1948 the Order of the Arrow became an official part of the national camping program of the Boy Scouts of America.

The Order of the Arrow recognizes those Scout campers who best exemplify the Scout Oath and Law in their daily lives. Its purpose is to promote Scout camping and the

Left: Scouts test their agility and endurance on this rugged course. *Above right and left, and below:* Scout Dale Yule and his dad, Scoutmaster Tom Yule, are seen here while on a troop hike in the vicinity of Crystal and Gray Wolf lakes, Montana.

development and maintenance of camping traditions and spirit. It intends to crystallize the Scout habit of helpfulness into a lifelong purpose of cheerful service to others.

The National Council of the Boy Scouts of America grants charters for local lodges of the Order of the Arrow to local councils. The acquisition of an Order of the Arrow lodge helps local councils to provide a quality Scouting program.

Today the OA has more than 164,000 members from over 400 local Boy Scouts of America councils. To be eligible for membership, a young man must be a registered Boy Scout, Varsity Scout or Explorer of First Class rank. He has experienced at least 15 days and nights of Scout camping, including a long-term camp. Membership in OA is by election of fellow unit members, following approval by the adult leader of the unit.

After election to OA, the Scout or Explorer goes through an induction ceremony called the Ordeal, conducted at Scout camp. This is the first step toward full membership. During the Ordeal, the inductee maintains complete silence, eats very little food, works on camp improvement projects and is required to sleep separately from other campers.

After he has given ten months of service, the inductee is invited to a Brotherhood ceremony. The ceremony further emphasizes the ideal of Scouting and the Order of the Arrow. After he has taken part in the Brotherhood cere-

Scouting ingenuity sometimes takes such interesting forms as this backwoods catapult *(above)*. *Right:* Scouting insignia and paraphernalia including an Order of the Arrow sash. *Overleaf:* A Scout-built bridge for the gymnastically inclined.

mony, the Scout is a full member of the Order of the Arrow.

Certain members of the Order of the Arrow may be recognized with the Vigil Honor for outstanding service to Scouting, his lodge and the community. He is eligible for this honor after two years as a Brotherhood member and with the approval of the Order of the Arrow Committee.

Six to twelve local lodges form an Order of the Arrow section. Once a year, representatives of the lodges convene for a conclave. Every two years all of the 57 elected section chiefs form the conference committee for the national Order of the Arrow conference.

A youth leader, called the region chief, is elected by the section chiefs for a two-year term of office. The election is held during the biennial meetings of section chiefs when they also elect the national chief and national vice-chief. These national officers preside at the national OA conference and serve two-year terms.

A professional advisor to the national Order of the Arrow committee is appointed by the chairman of the national Boy Scout committee to act as national executive secretary of the Order of the Arrow and to be a member of the national Boy Scout Division staff.

NATIONAL JAMBOREE

Among the many high adventures for eligible Scouts, a jamboree is tops. Twenty-eight thousand participants from 650 troops of Boy Scouts take part in a typical national Scout jamboree that lasts about a week. At a Scout jamboree, boys and leaders gain a clear understanding of and a deeper sense of commitment to the ideals of Scouting. The objective of the huge gathering is to celebrate the kind of healthy atmosphere that a large youth movement in a free society can make possible. A jamboree emphasizes the important need for physical fitness and for conservation of natural resources. Scouts at a jamboree take home with them new activities and Scout methods to share, so that even those Scouts unable to attend might benefit.

Boy Scouts who participate in a jamboree are selected by local councils whose choices are based on qualifica-

tions. Scouts chosen must have been active in a troop at least six months, are at least 12 years old but younger than 18 and have earned hiking, camping and cooking skill awards. They have filed personal health and medical records, have participated in prejamboree training experience and have been approved by their Scoutmaster or Varsity Scout coach and the local council.

Jamboree activities reflect Scouting skills, the nation's heritage, physical fitness, conservation and the spirit of brotherhood. Scouts demonstrate skills such as archery, boating, marksmanship and orienteering and practice new and tried methods in these and other skills. They can take part in updated versions of the handicapped aware-

Above: Comedian Herb Shriner gets a grip on knot-tying in rehearsal for the 1960 NBC special, *Jamboree. Opposite:* 'A Scout is Reverent': At a jamboree in Pennsylvania, Lutheran Council general secretary Dr Thomas Spitz Jr spoke to Protestant Scouts in a worship service (*upper left*); a young Scout follows the Jewish worship service (*upper right*); the Reverend Hogen Fujimoto (*lower left*) discusses plans for the Buddhist worship service; and Cardinal Terence Cooke accepts a gift during a Catholic worship service (*lower right*).

Left: These Scouts test their balance in a stump-high tug of war. *Above:* At a world jamboree, this Scout from Hong Kong gives a tip of the hat to fellow Scouts. *Below:* An Australian Scoutmaster helps one of his charges to master knot-tying.

ness trail, compete in events, participate in the arts and science fair and enjoy the merit badge midway. Scouts meet together in troop, intertroop and regional campfires and also at the opening and closing arena shows.

The jamboree site becomes a tent city of 28,000, with many normal 'city' services—bus system, telephones, hospital and first aid stations, postal service, food services, daily newspaper *(The Jamboree Journal)* and trading posts offering equipment, souvenirs, snacks, and photo services.

Religious services available to jamboree participants include Protestant, Roman Catholic, Mormon, Jewish, Eastern Orthodox, Christian Science, Lutheran, Episcopal, Friends, Reformed Latter Day Saints, Islamic, Buddhist, Unity and Unitarian Universalist among others. The participation of so many religious groups indicates the favorable partnership of the nation's religious community with the Boy Scouts of America. Chaplains from the various religious groups have either applied to serve at the jamboree or were invited by their religious groups to serve. At the jamboree chaplains lead religious services, visit sick participants and counsel Scouts and leaders.

On the jamboree's merit badge midway, Scouts have an opportunity to become acquainted with skills or hobbies that they may not have available at the local level. Many corporate, government and union organizations help to develop information about the more than 100 merit badge subjects for Boy Scouting, and at the jamboree these organizations provide qualified individuals, equipment and materials for the merit badge they are sponsoring. A Scout interested in earning one of the badges might be able to meet some of the requirements for the merit badge right at the jamboree and then complete them at home. The

International Scouting, *clockwise from above left:* **An Australian Venturer; Norwegian Scouts; Scouts under a tarp; and two Scouts of Kuwait exemplify Scouting diversity.** *Overleaf:* **Astronauts and former Scouts** *(starting at lower left)* **McNair(with glasses), McCandless, Stewart, Brand and Gibson.**

merit badges demonstrated at the 1985 jamboree included computers, farm mechanics, radio, railroading and stamp collecting, among many others.

The Boy Scouts of America promises three meals a day of top-quality food at a jamboree. To provide the more than one million meals takes over 600 people working in 22 warehouses and distribution centers, 20 field dining facilities and three cafeterias. Each scout at the jamboree also takes his turn at cooking on charcoal for his patrol. How does he know what to prepare? Luckily the jamboree committee adopts a menu that is easy to prepare and meets basic dietary requirements. Breakfasts are substantial. Lunches are for the trail and require no cooking. Dinners are hearty—beef stew, quarter-pound hamburgers, chicken a la king, etc.

With all their activity (and considering the appetites of teenaged boys) it's no surprise that Scouts at a jamboree eat 10 tons of breakfast cereal, 6 tons of granola bars, 5 tons of raisins, 15 tons of dried fruit and nuts and 400 gallons of mustard. They also consume 7½ tons of sirloin steak, 6 tons of bacon, 1½ tons of salami and 3 miles of link sausage!

At an international jamboree, all sorts of special dietary requests are made for a variety of reasons, and everything from Kosher foods to birthday cakes is provided for.

What about washing the dishes? Disposable plates and cups make cleanup simple. All that need to be washed are the pots, pans and tableware.

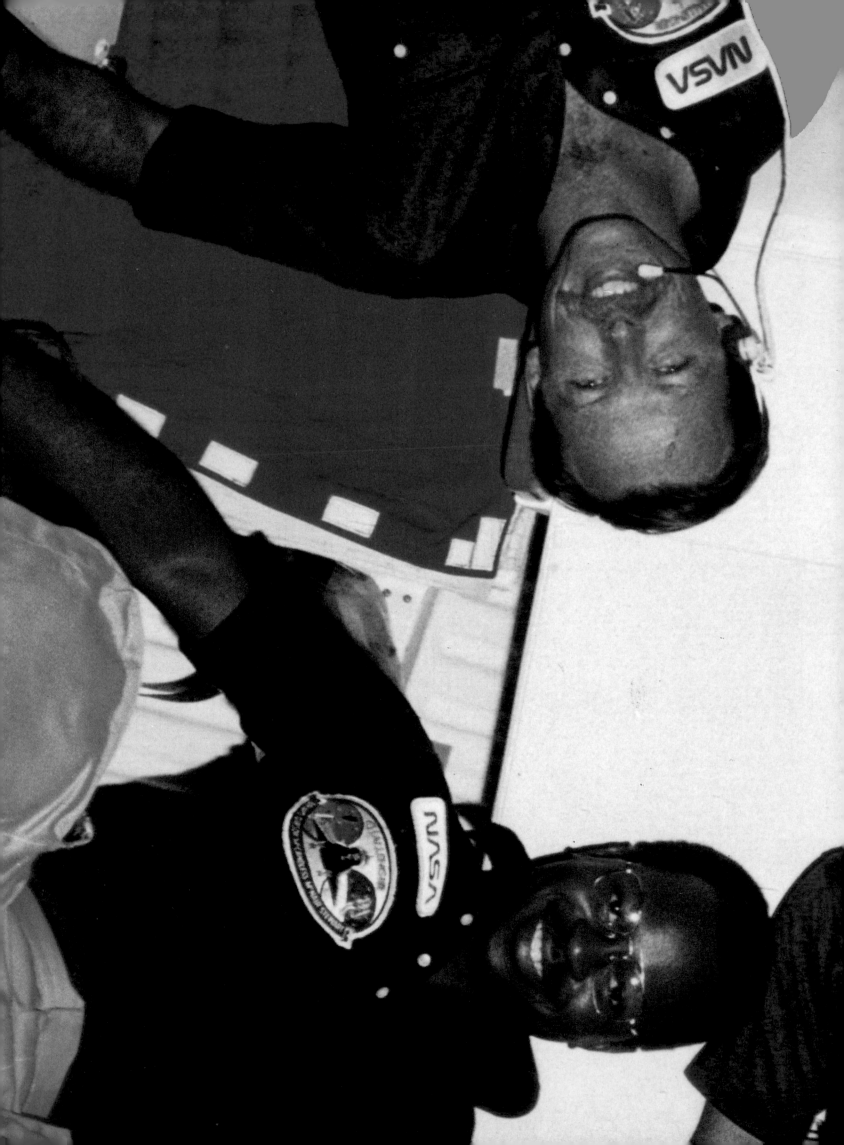

FORMER BOY SCOUTS

The Boy Scouts of America has touched the lives of a wide and very diverse group of individuals through its non-discriminatory membership policies, yet Scouting has produced some very special people. Among the 'celebrities' with Scouting backgrounds are actors, presidents, athletes and astronauts. These celebrities, as well as millions of other persons who may not be famous, have shown themselves to be fine citizens of their country.

For the past nine Congresses, the Boy Scouts of America has surveyed the members of the House and Senate regarding their participation in Scouting. The results of the most recent Congress Scouting survey show that sixty-four percent of congressional members had participated in Scouting. Eight members of the Senate earned Eagle Scout honors: Mark Andrews (North Dakota), Lloyd M Bentsen (Texas), Bill Bradley (New Jersey), Thad Cochran (Mississippi), Chic Hecht (Nevada), Richard G Lugar (Indiana), Sam Nunn (Georgia) and Warren Rudman (New Hampshire). Members of the House of Representatives boast even more Eagle Scouts: Gary L Ackerman (New York), Bill Alexander (Arkansas), Doug Barnard Jr (Georgia), Charles E Bennett (Florida), John Bryant (Texas), Bob Carr (Michigan), Jim Cooper (Tennessee), William E Dannemeyer (California), Hal Daub (Nebraska), John J Duncan (Tennessee), Thomas S Foley (Washington), Don Fuqua (Florida), Richard A Gephardt (Missouri), Dennis M Hertel (Michigan), John P Murtha (Pennsylvania), James R Olin (Virginia), Charles Pashayan Jr (California), Donald J Pease (Ohio), Claude D Pepper (Florida), J J Pickle (Texas), J Roy Rowland (Georgia), Eldon D Rudd (Arizona), Richard T Schulze (Pennsylvania), Philip R Sharp (Indiana), Ike Skelton (Missouri), Christopher H Smith (New Jersey), Robert F Smith (Oregon), Richard H Stallings (Idaho) and Gus Yatron (Pennsylvania).

Recipients of the Silver Beaver award are senators John Glenn (Ohio), Mark O Hatfield (Oregon), Sam Nunn (Georgia), and Malcolm Wallop (Wyoming) and representatives Albert G Bustamante (Texas), William F Gooding (Pennsylvania), Ike Skelton (Missouri), Floyd Spence (South Carolina) and George Wortley (New York).

Congressional recipients of the Silver Antelope are senators Wendell H Ford (Kentucky) and Mark O Hatfield (Oregon) and Representative George Wortley (New York).

Scouting teaches young people to be good citizens and trains them to become leaders. Embodying these qualities are many members of the astronaut program. Out of the 157 pilots and scientists selected as astronauts since 1959, over 90 were Scouts or active in Scouting. Among the Eagle Scout ranks are James C Adamson, Neil A Armstrong, James P Bagian, Guion S Bluford Jr, Gerald P Carr, Manley Lanier 'Sonny' Carter, Roger B Chaffee, Richard O Covey, John O Creighton, Charles M Duke Jr,

Top Left: **Apollo 11 astronauts Edwin Aldrin and Neil Armstrong are former Scouts, as were (*left, top to bottom*) Virgil Grissom, Edward White II and Roger Chaffee, who gave their lives in the Apollo 1 tragedy. *At right, clockwise from upper left:* Astronaut Guion S Bluford was a former Eagle Scout; as was Ellison S Onizuka, who died in the 1986 Space Shuttle tragedy. Astronaut Dale A Gardner was a First Class Scout.**

Donn F Eisele, Charles G Fullerton, S David Griggs, Jeffrey A Hoffman, Mark C Lee, Don L Lind, James A Lovell, Michael J McCulley, Bryan D O'Connor, Brian T O'Leary, Ellison S Onizuka, Elliot M See, Richard H Truly and David M Walker.

The diversity the individuals who have recounted Scouting backgrounds was noted by the Boy Scouts of America, who produced a public relations campaign that bore the images of famous persons who once were associated with Scouting. Among the celebrities was actor James Stewart, wearing his Scout uniform. It was an effective campaign for making the point that Boy Scouts grow up to be resourceful and contributing members of society. Some other celebrities with scouting backgrounds are Hank Aaron (baseball superstar), Milton Caniff (cartoonist), Dr William Devries (who transplanted the first artificial heart), George Evans (poet), Gerald Ford (the 38th President of the United States), David Hartman (television personality), Bruce Jenner (Olympic decathlon champion), Eddie Rabbitt (country and western singer), John Ritter (actor), Howard K Smith (former newscaster), Joe Theisman (athlete), Herschel Walker (athlete) and Paul Winfield (actor).

Some of these celebrities reached the highest achievements in Boy Scouting and others did not, but all were touched by Scouting—and their presence on the list above illustrates that Scouting is for everyone.

THE PRESIDENTS AND THE BOY SCOUTS

Since 1910, when William Howard Taft agreed to be the Honorary President of the Boy Scouts of America, each President of the United States has served as Honorary President during his term in office. Even before President Taft endorsed the Boy Scouts, Theodore Roosevelt (who was no longer President) was an ardent booster of the organization. To use his words, Teddy Roosevelt believed that the Boy Scout movement was 'one of the movements most full of promise for the future here in America.' He was the first council commissioner of Nassau County Council and became the first and only man designated to be 'Chief Scout Citizen.'

Woodrow Wilson signed the bill—passed in both houses of Congress by unanimous consent—granting federal incorporation to the Boy Scouts of America. President Wilson further stated, 'The Boy Scouts have not only demonstrated their worth to the nation, but have also materially contributed to a deeper appreciation by the American people of the higher conception of patriotism and good citizenship. . . . Anything that is done to increase the effectiveness of the Boy Scouts of America will be a genuine contribution to the welfare of the nation.'

In 1923, Warren G Harding authorized 'Harding Awards' to be given to 5000 Scout troops noting their increase in membership. President Harding commented, 'I am with the Scout movement heart and soul. It is an organization teaching the spirit of service and honor which we must always have in our citizenship. It is a school of democracy because in it, standing is won only by taking the equal opportunity given all individuals to show their own merit, capacity and worth. I wish every boy in our America could have the advantage and the honor of being in the Boy Scout organization.'

Calvin Coolidge had two sons who were Scouts and therefore had many opportunities to see Scouting in action. In 1926 President Coolidge presented the first Silver Buffalo awards. His comments: 'The more I have studied

Alan Shepard, Apollo 14 Moon mission (*far left*) commander, is a former First Class Scout. *Left:* President Dwight D Eisenhower was an avid Scout supporter. *Below:* Its sponsor, the 61st Infantry, inspects Cub Pack 64.

this movement, its inception, purposes, organization and principles, the more I have been impressed. Not only is it based on the fundamental rules of right thinking and acting, but it seems to embrace in its code almost every virtue needed in the personal and social life of mankind. It is a wonderful instrument for good.'

Herbert C Hoover launched a development program for the Boy Scouts of America at a dinner commemorating Scouting's 20th anniversary by saying, 'The first test of democracy is that each individual shall have the opportunity to take that position of leadership in the community to which his character, his ability and his ambition entitle him; and because of this the progress of our country is thus directly related to the training in leadership we can give the youth of the nation.'

Franklin D Roosevelt was the first President to enter the White House with a record as an active Scout leader. He was president of the Greater New York Councils of the Boy Scouts of America. When in 1934 President Roosevelt broadcast an appeal to help the needy, Scouts contributed by collecting nearly two million articles of clothing, furni-

68

ture, and other articles for needy families. 'As one who has been interested in Scouting over many years it has been most heartening to have so many evidences of the practical values of Scout training . . . [N]ext to active military service itself, there is no higher opportunity for serving our country than helping youth to carry on in their efforts to make themselves physically strong, mentally awake and morally straight, and prepared to help their country to the full in time of war, as well as in time of peace.'

Harry S Truman supported the Boy Scouts at every opportunity. He traveled to Valley Forge to personally open the Second National Jamboree in June 1950. He cited the Boy Scouts' great contribution 'to the character training of our youth.' He went on to say, 'What a greater nation this would be if the principles of Scouting could be woven more closely into our daily lives. If we can impress upon our youth principles of friendliness and mutual respect, we shall go a long way toward establishing a better understanding among the nations of the world. The Boy Scouts of America is making a vital contribution to the character building of our boys and young men. Let us work together to make the program of the Boy Scouts available to every American boy.'

Dwight D Eisenhower had been a staunch supporter of Scouting ever since his son was a Scout. He became a member of the national Executive Board of the Boy Scouts of America in 1948. During his term in the presidency he said: 'The Boy Scout movement merits the unstinting support of every American who wants to make his country and his world a better place in which to live. Its emphasis on community service and tolerance and world friendship promotes a speedier attainment of the enduring peace among men for which we all strive. By developing among its members both a spirit of sturdiness, self-reliance and a realization of the need for cooperative effort in every major enterprise, the movement is a prime force in preparing tomorrow's men for their duty to themselves, their country and their world.'

Above: Lyndon B Johnson was an active Eagle executive. *Below:* Texas Cub Scouts await John F Kennedy in 1963. *Upper right:* Troop 1 places a wreath on the Ernie Pyle Monument. *Lower right:* Then-governor Ronald Reagan received the Silver Beaver Award.

John F Kennedy was the first Scout to become President. He was a member of Troop 2, Bronxville, New York and a leader of the Boston Council. Kennedy said this of the Boy Scouts: 'For more than 50 years Scouting has played an important part in the lives of the Boy Scouts of this nation. It has helped to mold character, to form friendships, to provide a worthwhile outlet for the natural energies of growing boys and to train these boys to become good citizens of the future. In a very real sense, the principles learned and practiced as Boy Scouts adds to the strength of America and her ideals.'

Lyndon B Johnson was an active Scout leader in Austin, Texas, serving on an Exploring committee. In 1963 he helped to organize Post 1200 in Washington, DC, which was chartered to the House of Representatives for pages working in the US Congress. In doing so, President Johnson said, 'I welcome this opportunity to express my pride and deep sense of gratitude for the outstanding example and enviable reputation for human understanding and fair play which have throughout the productive life of your organization been hallmarks of Scouting everywhere. . . . As I applaud your past, I also urge you to rededicate yourselves to the ideals of the Scout Oath, and to reaffirm your obligations to your God and to your country. In so doing, you will contribute to the strengthening of America's heritage and thereby to the realization of our common goals in the Great Society.'

Above, left to right: **Chief Scout Executive Arthur Schuck and Scout Paul Eckman present Defense Secretary Thomas Gates with a scroll and a Norman Rockwell painting, on the BSA's 50th anniversary.** *Right:* **A 1943 visit to USAAF General 'Hap' Arnold.**

Richard M Nixon hosted the First National Explorer Presidents' Congress in 1971 on the White House lawn. He believed that 'Scouting offers an exceptional opportunity to learn about good citizenship by being a good citizen, and I am glad to hear that we can count on you to carry on the very important work . . . in encouraging America's boys to make themselves into the men our country needs.'

Gerald R Ford was the first Eagle Scout to become President. About that honor, President Ford said, 'One of the proudest moments of my life came in the Court of Honor when I was awarded the Eagle Scout badge. I still have that badge. It is a treasured possession. . . . The three great principles which Scouting provides—self-discipline, teamwork and moral and patriotic values—are the basic building blocks of leadership. I applaud the Scouting program for continuing to emphasize them. I am confident that your ability to bring ideals, values and leadership training to millions of our young people will help to bring about a new era—a time in which not only our Republic will progress in peace and freedom, but a time in which the entire world shall be secure, and all its people free.'

Jimmy Carter was a troop committee chairman, Explorer advisor, and Scoutmaster. The Boy Scouts held a Scouting Environment Day in 1977 in support of President Carter's appeal for an energy conservation program. President Carter said, 'As a former volunteer Scout leader . . . I am greatly impressed by the role of your fine program in our national life. It is a constructive initiative on the part of young Americans to explore career interests and to become better prepared for a more satisfying and rewarding future.'

Ronald Reagan, while serving as governor of California, became involved in Scouting with the Golden Empire Council in Sacramento. For his service to youth, he was awarded the Silver Beaver Award. He said to the Boy Scouts: 'I applaud your many efforts and programs en-

couraging character development and leadership among American youth. By sponsoring many useful physical, mental and social activities designed to promote self-responsibility, the Scouts strengthen the cornerstone of individual freedom in our nation. These programs develop the youngster's confidence in his ability to deal with nature, society and a challenging world.'

The Presidents have praised highly the Boy Scouts of America, but not surprisingly. The ideals of Scouting upon which some of them commented are the basis for the fine citizenship that Boy Scout of America encourages. Speaking as eloquently as each President's words is his service record of involvement with the Boy Scouts at local levels, for this is where the real effort of instilling Boy Scout ideals takes place.

SCOUTING IN CANADA

Similar to Boy Scouts worldwide, the Boy Scouts of Canada organization helps young people become responsible citizens. The aim of Boy Scouts of Canada is to help boys, youth and young adults to develop their character as resourceful and responsible members of the community. To work toward this goal, the Boy Scouts of Canada program provides opportunities and guidance for the mental, physical, social and spiritual development of its members.

The stated objectives of the Boy Scouts of Canada provide opportunities and guidance for its members to develop and demonstrate a personal understanding of God; the ability to accept responsibility for themselves and for the consequences of their actions; the ability to respond to others in caring ways; and awareness of and concern for the environment. Each program section emphasizes meeting these program objectives in ways appropriate to the age level of its members. The programs for all sections combine toward the development of the whole person, and work toward an in-depth appreciation and commitment to the principles of Scouting.

Scouting came to all parts of Canada in 1908, just months after Baden-Powell published the Boy Scout manual in England. The following anecdotes are two examples. As documented only by the recollections of persons who were present, one of the first Boy Scout troops in Canada was started in the backyard of a boy named Harris Neelon in St Catherines in 1908. Neelon himself was the leader of his troop. He had written to Baden-Powell for permission to form the troop, and it was himself who proclaimed the troop to be the first in Canada. Colorful recollections of the early days of Scouting in Canada have since that time been collected by the St Catherines District Scouts. The first camp, held in a grain field at Port Dalhousie, was attended by at least 20 boys. One of the endurance tests of that camp was to run barefoot over the stubble!

Another of the first Boy Scout troops in Canada formed in Merrickville in 1908. A Methodist minister, the Reverend Ernest Thomas, had traveled to England to learn about the Baden-Powell organization, and when he took up residence in Merrickville, he organized the first troop there—which predated the first troop in the United States by eight years. The Merrickville troop activities

Left: **This Canadian Scout squares off with a totem pole.** *Above:* **An Edmonton Boy Scout displays his patch blanket.**

were much the same as those of contemporary Scouts. They learned knot-tying, outdoor survival, fire-building and many of the other skills for which Boy Scouts everywhere are famous. In 1981 the troop leader of a new troop in Merrickville applied to the national organization for permission to call his troop 'The First Canada Troop,' thereby saving the memory of the 1908 troop from disappearing into oblivion. There are many such troops in Canada, and it is impossible to say which was 'The First.' Scouting existed for a year or more before local councils were formed, and four years before there was a national council. Since no records were kept, all such claimants are now recognized as simply being 'The First' in their community.

Canadian Parliament acted to incorporate the Boy Scouts of Canada on 12 June 1914. In 1918 the first issue of *Canadian Boy* appeared, and the same year dates the publication of the first Canadian Scout Handbook.

About 300 thousand young people belong to Canadian Scout units. The Boy Scouts of Canada national organization does not operate actual Beaver colonies, Cub packs, Scout troops, Venturer companies or Rover crews; it charters its program to such organizations as schools, churches, service clubs, professional and business associations, the Canadian Forces, institutions for disabled persons and other community groups. A separate organization, L'Association des Scouts du Canada, provides Scouting programs for French-speaking Canadian youth. These two Scouting organizations work closely together and both are headed by the Chief Scout of Canada—traditionally the Governor General of Canada.

The Boy Scouts of Canada sometimes calls itself Scouts Canada because it can be pronounced in English or in French. The affairs of Scouts Canada are administered and managed by an executive committee called the National Council. Scouts Canada grants charters to Provincial Councils to administer Scouting within an area defined by the charter, and Provincial Councils can also charter local councils to administer Scouting within defined areas. It is headquartered in Ottawa, Ontario.

Five age groups divide Canadian Scouts: Beavers, Wolf Cubs, Boy Scouts, Venturers and Rovers. Included in the programs of each group are considerations for special local conditions, such as exist within the Arctic communities, as well as the needs of ethnic groups or handicapped scouts.

Below: **Regional council patches change hands; below them are troop-identification jamboree patches.** *Right:* **A Vancouver, BC Scout is seen here aboard the Vancouver Island Ferry** *Victoria.* *Overleaf:* **A Canadian Cub explores a hollow log.**

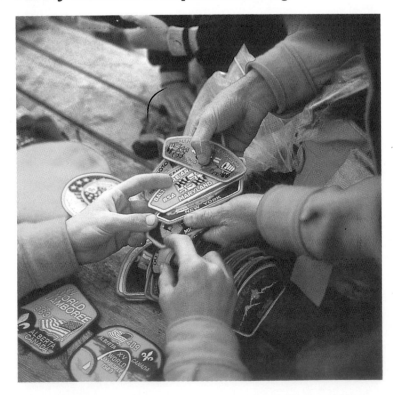

BEAVERS

Beavers are boys from five to seven years of age. Groups of about 20 to 25 boys form colonies. 1985 figures showed that about 80,000 Canadian boys belonged to Beaver colonies. Smaller groups within the colonies are called lodges and each is composed of five or six boys.

The Beaver uniform is blue and brown—which colors represent the sky and water, and the earth and the Beaver's coat. A Beaver wears a hat, a vest worn over his ordinary clothes and a neckerchief which he received when he is invested. At the time he is invested, a Beaver must know his Law, his Promise and the opening and closing ceremonies.

The Beaver Law is:
    A Beaver has fun, works hard,
    and helps his family and friends.

The Beaver Promise is:
    I promise to love God
    and to help take care of the world.

Above: A Scout at the 1983 World Jamboree in Alberta tries on headgear from the Far East. *Right:* Amid many mockups, seven Canadian Cubs with merit badges on their sleeves manhandle a Japanese motorcycle, at Vancouver's Expo '86.

Above: **This Vancouver, BC Scout pavilion, appears to the new arrival as a studiously crafted artifact of Canadian Indian 'architectural hieroglyphics.'** *Right:* **Compass orienteering is an important item on any Scout's wilderness agenda.**

No badges or awards are part of the Beaver program because the program strives to emphasize sharing rather than competition. The Beaver motto is 'Sharing, Sharing, Sharing.' A Beaver learns to share his belongings and his experiences. He learns through the examples of his leaders who share their role. One of their shared activities is the making of felt 'beaver tails' that they sew onto their hats. The color of the tail indicates the boy's age and degree of development as a Beaver. When the tail is changed every six months it indicates to the boy that he is growing and learning and able to do even better.

The emphasis of the Beaver program is on activities which help boys to find examples of God's love for them in the world and to experience and express love and joy. In expressing themselves, Beavers can enjoy good feelings about themselves. Their sense of cooperation through non-competitive activities helps to develop a sense of belonging and sharing. Their program activities help them enjoy, and therefore appreciate, the nature around them.

Beavers take their name from the story 'Friends of the Forest,' in which a family of beavers discovers a family of humans who are building a cottage down the creek from their pond. The Beaver program is based on this story—adopting terminology and names for the leaders from it, and adopting the concept of sharing which the story lends.

CUBS

Boys from 8 to 10 years old are organized into Cub packs. Packs are further divided into smaller units called sixes. Each six is led by a boy called a sixer, and each sixer usually has an assistant called a second. Sixes are known by colors and identify themselves by simple triangular patches in appropriate colors.

The Cub program emphasizes activities which help boys to express and respond to God's love in their daily lives. It encourages them to do their best and keep fit. It aims to satisfy their curiosity and need for adventure by providing new experiences that allow their creativity and sense of accomplishment to develop. Cubs make choices, develop a sense of fair play, and gather experience in being leaders. Their outdoor activities help them learn about the natural world and their responsibility to it.

Leaders of Cubs work in teams that strive to provide a balanced program of fun and activities in eight areas: acting, crafts, games, music, outdoor activities, star work, badge work and stories. The leadership team may consist of parents, other adults, teens and older Scouts who gather their pack for weekly meetings. One adult volunteer is the pack leader and has one assistant for every twelve boys.

To be invested as a Cub, a boy must know and understand his Promise, Law and motto.

The Cub Promise is:
   I promise to do my best,
   To do my duty to God and the Queen,
   To keep the law of the Wolf Cub Pack,
   And to do a good turn to somebody every day.

The Cub Law is:
   The Cub gives in to the Old Wolf
   The Cub does not give in to himself.

BOY SCOUTS OF CANADA AWARDS AND BADGES

FOR HIGH CHARACTER AND COURAGE

JACK CORNWELL DECORATION
...for high character and courage.

FOR GALLANTRY

BAR TO THE GOLD CROSS
For an additional and similar act of gallantry. (see gold cross)

GOLD CROSS
For gallantry, with special heroism and extraordinary risk.

BAR TO THE SILVER CROSS
For an additional and similar act of gallantry. (see silver cross)

SILVER CROSS
For gallantry, with considerable risk.

BAR TO THE BRONZE CROSS
For additional and similar act of gallantry. (see bronze cross)

BRONZE CROSS
For gallantry, with moderate risk.

Certificate for Gallantry awarded to

Boy Scouts of Canada

CERTIFICATE FOR GALLANTRY
For gallantry, with slight risk and worthy of recorded commendation.

FOR MERITORIOUS CONDUCT

BAR TO THE MEDAL FOR MERITORIOUS CONDUCT
For further meritorious conduct which would justify conferring a medal.

MEDAL FOR MERITORIOUS CONDUCT
For especially meritorious conduct not involving heroism or loss of life.

Certificate for Meritorious Conduct awarded to

Boy Scouts of Canada

CERTIFICATE FOR MERITORIOUS CONDUCT
For meritorious conduct worthy of recorded commendation but which does not justify a medal or a bar.

FOR OUTSTANDING SERVICE TO SCOUTING

SILVER FOX
For service of the most exceptional character to Scouting in the international field, performed by persons who are not members of Boy Scouts of Canada.

SILVER WOLF
For service of the most exceptional character to Scouting, normally of national importance.

BAR TO THE SILVER ACORN
For further especially distinguished service to Scouting.

THE SILVER ACORN
For especially distinguished service to Scouting.

BAR TO THE MEDAL OF MERIT
For further especially good service to Scouting.

MEDAL OF MERIT
For especially good service to Scouting.

MEDAL FOR GOOD SERVICE
For good service to Scouting.

Certificate of Commendation for service to Scouting awarded to

Boy Scouts of Canada

CERTIFICATE OF COMMENDATION
For service to Scouting worthy of commendation.

FOR LONG, FAITHFUL AND EFFECTIVE SERVICE

FOR ONE YEAR

FOR FIVE YEARS

FOR FIVE YEARS
for civies.

MEDAL FOR LONG SERVICE
For long, faithful and effective service to Scouting.
FOR TEN YEARS

ADDITIONAL PINS FIVE YEAR INTERVALS

83

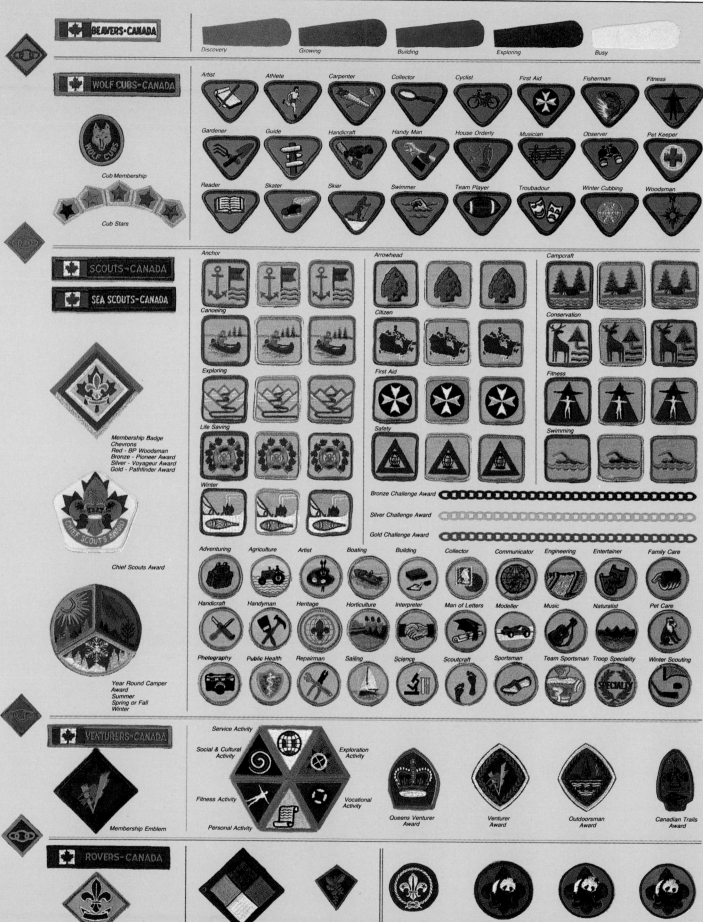

BEAVERS-CANADA

Discovery   Growing   Building   Exploring   Busy

WOLF CUBS-CANADA

Cub Membership

Cub Stars

Artist   Athlete   Carpenter   Collector   Cyclist   First Aid   Fisherman   Fitness

Gardener   Guide   Handicraft   Handy Man   House Orderly   Musician   Observer   Pet Keeper

Reader   Skater   Skier   Swimmer   Team Player   Troubadour   Winter Cubbing   Woodsman

SCOUTS-CANADA

SEA SCOUTS-CANADA

Membership Badge
Chevrons
Red - BP Woodsman
Bronze - Pioneer Award
Silver - Voyageur Award
Gold - Pathfinder Award

Chief Scouts Award

Year Round Camper
Award
Summer
Spring or Fall
Winter

Anchor   Arrowhead   Campcraft

Canoeing   Citizen   Conservation

Exploring   First Aid   Fitness

Life Saving   Safety   Swimming

Winter

Bronze Challenge Award
Silver Challenge Award
Gold Challenge Award

Adventuring   Agriculture   Artist   Boating   Building   Collector   Communicator   Engineering   Entertainer   Family Care

Handicraft   Handyman   Heritage   Horticulture   Interpreter   Man of Letters   Modeller   Music   Naturalist   Pet Care

Photography   Public Health   Repairman   Sailing   Science   Scoutcraft   Sportsman   Team Sportsman   Troop Speciality   Winter Scouting

VENTURERS-CANADA

Membership Emblem

Service Activity
Social & Cultural Activity   Exploration Activity
Fitness Activity   Vocational Activity
Personal Activity

Queens Venturer Award   Venturer Award   Outdoorsman Award   Canadian Trails Award

ROVERS-CANADA

Rover Membership

Rover Badge   Rover Rambler

World Scout Badge   World Conservation Badge

Religion in Life

Above: These Scouts are wearing pink jamboree tags, and very sober expressions. *Right:* This Newfoundland 'Killick' or stone anchor was the focus of a Beaver contest. *Far right:* A North Saskatchewan-Council Scout, wearing a round badge with glyphs symbolizing the various activities in which he specializes. *Overleaf:* 'Be Prepared.' A Scoutmaster and his troop gain experience with this taste of 'all-weather camping.'

The Cub motto is 'Do your best.'

Cubs continue the sharing emphasis of Beavers by playing and learning in groups, but at the same time can earn up to 25 badges and five stars for their individual achievements. Cubs may wear their stars and badges on their gray uniforms with a yellow and green neckerchief.

SCOUTS

Boys from 11 to 14 years of age form troops of 20 to 30 members. A volunteer adult works with the troop as Troop Scouter and has one assistant (Scout Counsellor) for every one or two patrols—the smaller groups within the troop. Scouts usually attend weekly meetings in patrols which usually have from five to eight members. One Scout is elected by his patrol to be Patrol Leader. The leadership in the patrol can move from Scout to Scout depending on their activities or projects.

To be invested as a Scout, a boy must know his Promise, Law and motto.

The Scout Promise is:
> On my honour, I promise to do my best,
> To love and serve God, my Queen, my Country and
>   my fellow men,
> and to live by the Scout law.

The Scout Law is:
> A Scout is helpful and trustworthy,
> kind and cheerful,
> considerate and clean,
> wise in the use of his resources.

The Scout motto is 'Be Prepared.'

The Scout program emphasizes activities which help boys to behave in ways that show their concern for others and their understanding of God. It helps them develop self reliance and encourages them to pursue hobbies and personal interests. It aims to develop self discipline and skills for working cooperatively with other people in setting and achieving patrol and personal goals. The program encourages its members to practice leadership skills, to relate with adults and to be of service to others. It emphasizes camping, exploring the outdoors and developing good conservation practices.

In this age group, boys begin to develop their physical fitness and leadership skills in outdoor activities. They go on camping trips where they learn outdoor cooking, hiking, swimming and first aid. Their outdoor activities stress their harmony with their environment while they enjoy it, and many of their indoor activities stress acquiring the skills for successful outdoor activities.

Scouts work toward 13 achievement badges and 31 challenge badges. Achievement badges are pursued by patrols, and each badge has three levels so that a patrol can work at a level which is a reasonable challenge for them. The challenge badges focus on individual hobbies and interests and are earned by individual Scouts. Other awards such as the Chief Scouts' Award are also available to boys who earn them.

Scouts wear dark green shirts, navy blue trousers and red plaid neckerchiefs.

VENTURERS

Teenagers from 14 to 17 years of age form companies of Venturers. They may be boys or girls.

The Venturer program emphasizes activities which help its members to show that they care and live according to their personal values and religious beliefs. It encourages the development and use of skills in communicating, solving problems and making decisions. It stresses the exploration of vocational opportunities and encour-

ages its members to participate in a variety of social, cultural and spiritual activities. It allows opportunities for leadership and to work cooperatively in adult-like situations. The program, which includes challenging physical and outdoor activities, helps its members to become aware of the needs of the community and the environment, and to respond to those needs.

Venturer advisors are recruited by the sponsoring organization. Advisors may be parents or other adults who provide a wide range of projects and activities. If the group is coeducational, it is desirable to have coeducational leadership.

Venturers usually attend weekly meetings in a group called a company, consisting of from five to eight members. Rarely does a company exceed twelve members. The company elects an executive from among its membership to handle administrative functions, but any member may be appointed to lead specific activities or projects.

To become a Venturer, a young person must know and understand the Venturer promise:

On my honour
I promise to develop myself
so that I may better love and serve God,
respect and help my fellow man,
honour and render service to my country.

The Venturer motto is 'Challenge.'

Left: **Perhaps the photographer has caused the typical boyish awkwardness in these valiant fishermen.** *Below:* **Heads up, heads down—there's more than one way to cross a bridge!** *Right:* **Scouts with an agricultural bent practice branding.**

Many Venturer activities place an emphasis on living in the outdoors and enjoying the environment in harmony with nature. Camping, hiking, outdoor cooking and other outdoor activities are popular. Certain activities, such as camping in the snow or ice fishing, may be available to Venturer companies because of their geographic region. These same activities might not be available to other Venturers, but the important concept of living with nature without harming the environment is shared by all Venturers, as well as by all Scouts throughout the world.

Venturer companies usually remain small, and it is not uncommon or unacceptable for a company to enjoy its formation for only a few years before its demise when its members leave. Other companies can be formed in the group, each with its own life cycle.

Increasingly popular Venturer companies are those which are oriented to the vocational, such as Police Venturing.

Venturers wear tan shirts, blue trousers and dark green ties.

ROVERS

Young adults from 18 to 26 years of age, both male and female, may join a Rover group. The group provides opportunities for individual development and a chance to explore various careers. The Rover program shares the aim of Scouts Canada and other programs to help develop character in its members as resourceful and responsible members of the community. It encourages

These Canadian Scouts deepen their agricultural interest by feeding the chickens—with a lot of flair!

Left: **Venturers share a laugh while planning an outing.** *Above:* **A Canadian Venturer explains Scouting pins at a jamboree.**

this development by providing opportunities and guidance for its members' mental, physical, social and spiritual development.

In its activities, the Rover program tries to help young adults to develop spiritual depth and joy in living while establishing their own sense of identity, values and life styles. It encourages them to become self-directed individuals and responsible adult members of society at large while, at the same time, they blend personal freedom with group responsibility. Participation in the Rover program offers its members the chance to develop meaningful and lasting friendships and to provide meaningful services to the community. As with all Scout Canada programs, its members participate in satisfying outdoor activities that contribute to protection of the environment, fitness and a sense of well-being.

Rover advisors may be parents or other adults recruited by the sponsoring organization who work with the members to provide a wide range of projects and activities. Rovers usually attend weekly meetings in a group called a crew. A crew typically has from five to eight members and, if it is a coeducational crew, desires to have both male and female advisors.

SCOUTING IN THE UNITED KINGDOM

The Scout Association United Kingdom, whose membership totals 650,000 Scouts and Scouters, keeps its headquarters at Baden-Powell House in London. This address is particularly appropriate because Lord Baden-Powell founded the Scout Movement in that city.

Scouting for Boys was published in 1908, a year after Baden-Powell's experimental camp for boys was held on Brownsea Island, and after several years of development in consultation with men whose opinions Baden-Powell admired.

The Scouting Movement soared. It gathered boys from throughout England—boys from all social classes were eager to become Scouts. When even girls wanted to join the Scouts Movement, the Girl Guide Movement evolved.

Robert Baden-Powell, or 'BP', devoted the rest of his life to Scouting. So much of the present day Scout terminology and customs came directly from Baden-Powell, it is difficult to recount them. Among the many words he coined is 'jamboree,' now recognized the world over by even non-Scouts, a symbol of Scouting's brotherhood of goodwill and fun.

Baden-Powell established the Boy Scouts in the United Kingdom, and the organization continues to uphold Baden-Powell's original ideals as it strives to continue its appeal to contemporary boys.

Boy Scouts in the United Kingdom were the model for all the other organizations in other countries, but each country's specific age divisions may be different today. The Scout Association United Kingdom includes about 80,000 adult volunteer Scouters for a total membership of 650,000.

Northern Ireland is the only part of the United Kingdom that offers boys from ages 6 to 8 an opportunity to become Scouts. They may join as Beaver Scouts. Activities for these young boys are similar to the activities of Beavers in Canada or Tiger Cubs in the United States.

Boys from 8 to 11 years of age throughout the United Kingdom can become Cub Scouts. Recent figures show them to be 300,000 members strong. Cubs partake of the Boy Scout traditions of outdoor activities and personal development.

UK Scouts at the 15th World Jamboree shared smiles (*left*) and conversations (*right*) with brother Scouts from other lands.

Boys from 11 to 15 years of age can become Boy Scouts. Approximately 220,000 boys of this age presently are members of the Boy Scouts.

Young adults from 15 to 20 can become Venturers. There are about 25,000 Venturers in the United Kingdom who enjoy outdoor activities such as rowing and hiking besides investigating various careers. In certain countries Venturers may include men and women up to 30 years of age.

Above: The entry gate to the 1967 World Jamboree was built in the form of a Japanese ceremonial gate. Present at that same jamboree, the United Kingdom's large contingent wore traditional clothing *(below). Right:* Jamboree cricket!

Left: Living in lands so steeped in traditional crafts and folklore as the British Isles, UK Scouts have a unique opportunity to explore ancient European arts via 'hands-on' training. These Scouts *at left* are learning to tool leather, an old and honored craft connected with the saddler's art. UK Scouts often attend international Scouting jamborees like the 15th World Jamboree held in Canada *(above)*. Being at home wherever you go is precisely what Scouting in the UK is about—brotherhood, camaraderie and knowing that in other shires, countries and places that may seem like entirely different worlds, the UK Scout of today always has many brothers *(below). Overleaf:* Part of attending jamborees is helping to construct and put to use various rustic edifices—such as this rope bridge, upon which UK Scouts (among others) have a chance to try their derring-do.

ROBERT BADEN-POWELL

Robert Stephenson Smyth Baden-Powell was born on 22 February 1857 in London. He was the twelfth child of his father, a professor, and the eighth child of his mother, the professor's third wife. When Robert was but three years old his father died.

Robert's high idealism showed itself when he was only eight years old. Writing in his diary a set of 'Laws for Me When I am Old,' he began, 'I will have the poor people to be as rich as we are, and they ought by rights to be as happy as we. . . .'

His idealism led him to seek a commission in the Army in 1876. He joined the thirteenth Hussars in India as a Second Lieutenant at the age of 19. His military career developed and Baden-Powell continued to share his own ideas by writing them down. In 1884 when he was in South Africa he wrote the first of his published books, *Reconnaissance and Scouting*, based on his reconnaissance experience in the Drakensberg Mountains.

In 1885, only nine years after he had joined the Army, Baden-Powell was given command of the 13th Hussars. The next year, while observing Russia and Germany on maneuvers, Baden-Powell was put under open arrest but escaped and returned to South Africa. In 1886 during the campaign against Dinizulu, Baden-Powell first heard the tribal song 'Eengonyama Gonyama!' which later appeared in *Scouting for Boys*.

By 1895, when Baden-Powell was raising a native contingent for scouting and pioneering in the Ashanti expedition against King Prempeh, he had begun wearing the large-brimmed hat that was to later become the Scout hat. After successful work in the Ashanti campaign, for which he earned promotion, Baden-Powell took on the Matabele campaign, during which he earned the nickname 'Impeesa' ('the wolf that never sleeps') from the tribesmen.

The next year Baden-Powell took command of the 5th Dragoon Guards in India. In India he awarded his men with arm badges of fleur-de-lis, now familiar to Scouts all over the world.

In 1899 Baden-Powell again went to South Africa. There he raised two regiments of mounted infantry and organized the defense of the Rhodesian and Bechuanaland frontiers against the Boers. His general supply center during the Boer War was the town of Mafeking. Two days after the war began, Mafeking was surrounded and the famous Siege of Mafeking began. After 217 days Baden-Powell was relieved by British forces. He overnight was hailed as the 'Hero of Mafeking' for he and his 800 men (aided

Left: Lord and Lady Baden-Powell are shown here on 9 June 1932 at Camp Albury Park, Surrey, in southern England. *Above:* This photo was taken shortly after their marriage in 1912. The Scouting founder's hard-working wife eventually rose to the position of Chief of the Girl Guide movement.

by a Cadet Corps of young boys) had withstood the long siege against thousands of Boers. He was promoted to Major-General (the youngest General in the Army at age 43) and was celebrated all over the British Empire. One war correspondent for the *London Morning Post* who interviewed Baden-Powell was the young Winston Churchill.

He was a celebrity. He had reached the top of his career (he thought!). In 1904 Baden-Powell went through a period of crisis, unsure of what to do or how to use his fame in the best way. William Smith, the founder of the Boys' Brigade (a youth organization whose purpose was instilling discipline in boys), made a suggestion to Baden-Powell that later changed the world. He challenged Baden-Powell to think up ways to make the Boys' Brigade attractive to more boys, suggesting something based on *Aids to Scouting*, the manual that Baden-Powell had written for his men in the army.

Above: A British Boy Scout converses with the second American in orbit, astronaut Scott Carpenter, at an international jamboree. *Below:* Honoring proud British Isles tradition, these UK Scouts wear kilts, as also do these Scouts *at right.*

CONCLUSION

The international Scouting Movement that Robert Baden-Powell began in 1907 has influenced many generations of people in all parts of the world. His Movement continues today—in full force 80 years after it started. The opportunities for participation that Scouting offers to young men and young women have increased over the years. Scouting activities have been modified to keep the interests of contemporary boys and young adults, and its uniforms have undergone many changes. What has remained constant, however, are the guiding principles of respect for God, service to others and striving for personal development. Boy Scouting today is therefore not drastically different from Boy Scouting of long ago. Boy Scouting has kept what was good and modified its program for wider opportunities for all young people, no matter where they live, what color they are, which creed they follow or how gainly their step. To develop themselves to the best of their ability, to be good citizens of their countries and to serve their God honorably—that's what Boy Scouting today is all about.

Left: **Arizona Cubs and (***being bandaged***) their first aid advisor.**
Right: **A papier mache Statue of Liberty 'torches' a papier mache crow as Cub Scouts look on.** *Below:* **Young Scouts on a rainy walk.**
Overleaf: **Scouts of every kind have a focus—and red woolen jackets—in common at this world jamboree.**

Members of the World Organization and their membership*

Country	Members	Country	Members	Country	Members
Algeria (2)	72,801	Guatemala (5)	12,045	Pakistan (3)	207,196
Argentina (5)	23,856	Guyana (5)	532	Panama Rep. (5)	2308
Armenian Scouts (4)	1112	Haiti (5)	15,341	Papua New Guinea (3)	1828
Australia (3)	170,927	Honduras (5)	1779	Paraguay (5)	4051
Austria (4)	21,002	Hong Kong (3)	42,830	Peru (5)	15,511
Bahamas (5)	1625	Iceland (4)	4698	Philippines (3)	2,364,541
Bahrain (2)	1845	India (3)	709,754	Portugal (4)	32,421
Bangladesh (3)	185,005	Indonesia (3)	2,347,164	Qatar (2)	5136
Barbados (5)	3349	Iran (3)	105,515	Rwanda (1)	6935
Belgium (4)	81,679	Iraq (2)	11,319	Saudi Arabia (2)	17,370
Benin (1)	6961	Ireland (4)	57,386	Senegal (1)	6123
Bolivia (5)	3887	Israel (4)	26,760	Sierra Leone (1)	4800
Botswana (1)	4979	Italy (4)	88,854	Singapore (3)	12,427
Brazil (5)	47,565	Ivory Coast (1)	6436	South Africa (1)	37,489
Brunei (3)	2134	Jamaica (5)	9090	Spain (4)	58,524
Burkina Faso (1)	10,128	Japan (3)	323,128	Sri Lanka (3)	20,121
Burundi (1)	1833	Jordan (2)	14,751	Sudan (2)	13,550
Cameroon (1)	6973	Kenya (1)	55,225	Surinam (5)	2531
Canada (5)	308,696	Korea (3)	280,213	Swaziland (1)	1388
Central African Rep. (1)	7000	Kuwait (2)	8296	Sweden (4)	100,752
Chad (1)	4000	Lebanon (2)	9000	Switzerland (4)	43,141
Chile (5)	34,861	Lesotho (1)	371	Syria (2)	11,073
China, Boy Scouts of (3)	87,522	Liberia (1)	4973	Tanzania (1)	12,356
Colombia (5)	13,651	Libya (2)	9010	Thailand (3)	457,389
Costa Rica (5)	4404	Liechtenstein (4)	718	Togo (1)	6040
Cyprus (4)	3321	Luxembourg (4)	4780	Trinidad-Tobago (5)	23,160
Denmark (4)	50,723	Madagascar (1)	6460	Tunisia (2)	27,981
Dominican Rep. (5)	4100	Malaysia (3)	84,908	Turkey (4)	16,031
Ecuador (5)	1785	Malta (4)	1207	Uganda (1)	13,982
Egypt (2)	50,002	Mauritania (2)	1852	United Arab Emirates (2)	4160
El Salvador (5)	5926	Mauritius (1)	4865	United Kingdom (4)	614,622
Ethiopia (1)	9829	Mexico (5)	41,323	United States (5)	4,155,708
Fiji (3)	7291	Monaco (4)	127	Uruguay (5)	1507
Finland (4)	35,580	Morocco (2)	11,918	Venezuela (5)	23,574
France (4)	114,861	Nepal (3)	35,135	Yemen (Arab) (2)	6601
Gabon (1)	4735	Netherlands (4)	53,071	Zaire (1)	44,063
Gambia (1)	7808	New Zealand (3)	60,090	Zambia (1)	3099
Germany, Fed. Rep. (4)	131,065	Nicaragua (5)	1484	Zimbabwe (1)	6494
Ghana (1)	13,192	Nigeria (1)	48,479		
Greece (4)	30,514	Norway (4)	23,240		
Grenada (5)	581	Oman (2)	3500	World Scout Bureau	36

Scouting is also active in these other countries and territories:

Anguilla, Antigua, Ascension Island, Belize, Bermuda, Bhutan, British Virgin Island, Cayman Island, Comoro Island, Cook Island, Dominica, Djibouti, Faroe Island, French Guiana, French Polynesia, Gambia, Gibraltar, Greenland, Guadeloupe, Guam, Kiribati, Malawi, Maldive Is., Martinique, Montserrat, Nauru, Netherlands Antilles, New Caledonia, Niger, Reunion, St Helena, St Kitts/Nevis, St Lucia, St Pierre & Miquelon, St Vincent, Seychelles, Solomon Island, Tokelau Island, Tonga, Tristan da Cunha, Turks & Caicos Island, Tuvalu, Vanuatu, Western Samoa.

(1) Africa Region   (2) Arab Region   (3) Asia-Pacific Region   (4) European Region   (5) Inter-American Region

*Membership figures from World Scouting Fact Sheet, November 1985.

INDEX

A

Aids to Scouting for N-COs and Men: 7, 103
Arrow of Light Award: 28
Australian Scouts: 17

B

Baden-Powell, Agnes: 8
Baden-Powell, Olave: 8, *102-103*
Baden-Powell House: 95
Baden-Powell, Robert Stephenson Smyth: *7, 8, 17, 21, 73, 95, 102-103*, 107
Beard, Daniel Carter: 21
Beaver Scouts (Canada): 74, 78-80
Beaver Scouts (Northern Ireland): 101
The Birch Bark Roll: 21
Bobcats: 26
Boer War: 7, 103
Boy Scouts (Canada): 74, 84-85
Boy Scouts (United Kingdom): 95
Boy Scouts of America: 21-22
Boy Scouts of Canada (see also Scouts Canada): 74
Boyce, William D: 7, 21
Boy's Brigade: 7, 103
Boys Life: 14, 22
Bronze Palm: 34
Brownsea Island camp: 7, 21, 95

C

Canadian Boy: 74
Canadian Scout Handbook: 74
Career Awareness Exploring: 34, 38
Churchill, Winston: 103
Cub Scout Promise: 25-26
Cub Scouts (United Kingdom): 95

E

Eagle Scout: 32-34, 39
Eagle Scout Badge: 32
Eagle Scout Challenge: 32
Eagle Scout Palms: 34
Edson, Carroll A: 49
Edward VII: 8
Elizabeth II: 8
Everett, P W: 7
Explorer Presidents' Association Congress: 22

Exploring: 38
Exploring for the Handicapped: 48

F

First Class Scouts: 32
Former Boy Scouts
    Astronauts: *62-64, 66*-67
    Celebrities: *20, 57, 66*
    Representatives: 64
    Senators: 64

G

Gates, Thomas: *70*
George V: 8
Gilwell Park: 8
Girl Guides (see also Girl Scouts): 8, 101
Girl Scouts (see also Girl Guides): 8
Goodman, Dr E Urner: 49
Gold Arrow: 26-28
Gold Palm: 34
Green, G W: 7

H

Handicap Awareness Newsletter: 48
Handicapped Awareness Trail: 48
Handicapped Service: 42
Harding Awards: 67

J

The Jamboree Journal: 60

K

Kandersteg International Camp: 14
King's Scout Badge: 8

L

Lake George, NY camp: 21
L'Association des Scouts du Canada: 74
Law Day: 34
Law of the Pack: 26
Life Scout: 32
Lone Scout Medallion: 41
Lord Edward Cecil's Cadet Corps: 7

M

Mason, Charlotte: 7
Mafeking, Siege of: 7, 103

N

National Advisory Committee on Scouting for the Handicapped: 42
National Boy Scout Division: 52
National Court of Honor: 34
National Council: 22, 52
National Eagle Scout Association: 22
Neelon, Harris: 73
Northern Ireland: 95
Nyeri, Kenya: 8

O

The Official Boy Scout Handbook: 42, 48-49
Ordeal: 52
Order of the Arrow: 22, 49-52
Order of the Arrow Committee: 52
Order of the Arrow Conference: 52

P

Poole Harbour: 7

Q

Queen's Scout Badge: 8

R

Reconnaissance and Scouting: 103
Relationships Division: 42
Robson, H: 8
Rovers (Canada): 74, 89-93

S

Scout Association United Kingdom: 95
Scout Life Guard: 34
Scout Law: 7, 8, 22, 32, 49
Scout Motto: 8, 22
Scout Oath (see also Scout Promise): 22, 32, 49
Scout Promise (see also Scout Oath): 7, 8, 22
Scout Sign: 13
Scout Slogan: 8, 22
Scouting: 22
Scouting Environment Day: 71
Scouting for Boys: 7, 21, 95, 103
Scouting for the Handicapped: 14, 48

Scouts Canada (see also Boy Scouts of Canada): 74
Sea Scouts: 38, *39*
Second Class Scouts: 32
Seton, Ernest Thompson: 21
Silver Antelope Award: 64
Silver Arrow: 26-28
Silver Beaver Award: 64
Silver Buffalo Award: 67
Silver Palm: 34
Smith, Sir William: 7, 103
Sons of Daniel Boone: 21
Star Scout: 32

T

Tenderfoot Scouts: 32
Thomas, the Reverend Ernest: 73
Tiger Cub Scouts: 26
Treasure Island Camp: 49

U

Understanding Cub Scouts with Handicaps: 48
Understanding Scouts with Handicaps: 48
United States Foundation for International Scouting: 14
United States Olympic Committee: 38
United States Presidents: 21, *66-68*, 70-72

V

Varsity Scout Pledge: 41
Venturers (Canada): 74, 85-89
Venturers (United Kingdom): 95
Vigil Honor: 52

W

Webelos Badge: 28
Webelos Scouts: 28
West, Dr James E: 21, 42
Wolf Badge: 26
Wolf Cubs (Canada): 74, 80-84
The Woodcraft Indians: 21
World Friendship Fund: 13-14
World Jamborees: 15-17
World Scout Bureau: 13
World Scout Committee: 13
World Scout Conference: 13, 22

Acknowledgements

Many thanks to Bob Milks, Don Olson and Mike Roytek for their words of encouragement, and to Lillian Castillo-Speed for her help. Special thanks to Mr Kerry D Kirkland, without whose generous assistance this book would not have been possible.

Photo Credits

Bob Allen: 27, 107 (upper right)
American Graphic Systems Archives: 48
Baden-Powell House: 7, 102, 103
Boy Scouts of Canada: 72, 75, 76-77, 78-79, 81, 82, 85, 88, 90-91, 92-93
Catholic Archdiocese of San Francisco: 33, 44 (lower left), 44-45, 56 (all)
Church of Jesus Christ of Latter-Day Saints: 6, 9, 10-11, 12, 13, 14 (upper left), 14-15, 16, 17, 18-19, 20, 22, 23, 30-31, 40, 41 (left and right), 46 (upper and lower left), 46-47, 50, 53 (upper right and bottom), 54-55, 58-59, 59 (upper and lower right), 60 (left and right), 61 (top and bottom), 73, 74 (lower left), 78 (upper left), 80, 83 (left and right), 84, 89 (left and right), 91 (upper left), 93 (upper left), 94-95, 97, 98, 99 (top and bottom), 100-101, 105, 107 (bottom), 108-109, 112
The Cinema Shop: 57
Raymond L DeLeon: 34, 35, 38, 42, 91 (lower left)

© Kerry D Kirkland: 52, 53 (upper left)
Lyndon B Johnson Space Center: 65 (upper right)
NASA: 8, 62-63, 64 (top and bottom), 65 (upper left and bottom), 68 (bottom), 96 (top and bottom), 104 (top and bottom)
National Archives: 49, 98
National Maritime Museum: 39
Reynolds Aluminum: 26
Karl H Schumacher, the White House: 69 (bottom)
The United Way: 24, 29, 43, 102 (lower right), 106
US Air Force: 28, 68 (top), 71
US Department of Defense: 25, 32, 36-37, 67, 69 (top), 70
© Bill Yenne: 66 (right)
© Tom R Yule: 51 (upper left, upper right, bottom), 86-87

Overleaf: **The openess of this Scout's face belongs to any age, and to any location: whether in forest, city or tiny town, the Scout is at home and ready for any eventuality. Ever cognizant of the fact that he lives not only in the international brotherhood of Scouting, but also that he lives in the vast family of humanity, he can be called upon to do a 'Good Turn' in any situation. Even the youngest Scout is guided to 'Be Prepared.'**

Knit Toys

Knit Toys

NATHALIE CRAIG

ARCO PUBLISHING, INC.
NEW YORK

Copy-1

Published by Arco Publishing, Inc.
215 Park Avenue South, New York, N.Y. 10003

Copyright © 1985 by Nathalie Craig

Library of Congress Cataloging in Publication Data

Craig, Nathalie.
  Knit toys.

  1. Knitting.   2. Soft toy making.   I. Title.
TT825.C73 1985   745.592′4   84-28341
ISBN 0-668-06268-1 (cloth)

Printed in the United States of America
10 9 8 7 6 5 4 3 2 1

To my husband, Elden—
for always understanding
my love of needlework
instead of housework.

Contents

Acknowledgments

To the many people who helped shape this book from a dream into reality—my sincere thanks. They include:

My daughter-in-law, Beth, who typed and helped proofread every word.

My grandchildren, Christine and Daniel, who are a constant inspiration for toymaking.

Mason Philip Smith, the photographer, whose pictures bring all my toys and dolls to life.

And—my editors, Sandy Towers and Paula Reedy, for much help and patience extended to a first-time author.

Introduction

It seems children of all ages, including grown-up ones, like dolls and stuffed animals. They're often so appealing that somehow we can't resist picking them up or even hugging them. For this book I have designed many stuffed toys of all sizes (including dolls both big and little) that are not only fun to admire, own, and play with, but fun to make.

All the toys in this book are knitted and then finished and dressed with various fabrics and trims. Some of the clothes are "knit-on" as you go; others are added later. Only the simplest of knitting stitches are used, so the toys are as easy to make for a beginning knitter as for an experienced one. Many grandmothers and aunts who would love to make a new bear, doll, or bunny for a favorite child would doubtless also be happy to share their knitting know-how with beginners. How much fun it would be for a little girl to learn to knit by making her own new doll!

The yarns I have used are easily obtained acrylics of knitting worsted size. Since only small amounts are needed (especially small for the smaller toys), the person who knits regularly will probably have enough left-over yarn to make almost everything. If this isn't the case or if you're a beginner, ask around—your friends may be glad to share their leftovers with you. Fabric, felt, and trims are likewise needed only in the quantities that may be found in most sewing baskets. This is a good opportunity to be imaginative and use up whatever is available. If you *must* buy yarn and materials, the cost will not be high if you take advantage of sales or buy remnants. Remember that the materials and yarn will go a long way, and this helps to keep the costs to a minimum.

So, please, go ahead, pick out your favorite and try it. You'll be surprised how easy it is to knit these toys and how quickly you're finished. There's something here for everyone: little cats and dogs, soft bunnies for babies, little bears for little boys, sweet dolls for sweet little girls— toys to please everyone. Just watch the smiles appear when you give one to your favorite child. These toys are sturdy enough to be really played with. The little dolls and bears can even be used in a large-sized doll house, or hung on the Christmas tree.

Don't forget to try these dolls and toys for fund-raisers or bazaars. Their low cost and winning appeal will make them profitable items.

Above all, may you enjoy this book and have fun with these dolls and toys. Perhaps they will inspire you to experiment and design some of your own!

Some General Directions and Helpful Hints

The materials and needles needed for each individual project are given at the beginning of every set. There are, however, some general tools and equipment you will need. They are:

Tracing paper for patterns
Pencil
Scissors both for paper and fabric
Ruler and/or tape measure
Yarn markers (or use contrasting yarn)
Stitch counter
Cardboard (to wind yarn around to make hair)
Tapestry (yarn) needle
Pins and pin cushion

Each toy or set of toys is given with complete instructions for knitting, assembling, sewing together, and then dressing or decorating. There are full-sized patterns for the features and clothing. The seam allowances, where needed, are always provided for—so trace and cut out the patterns and materials exactly as instructed.

If you read the book through, it may seem as though some instructions are repeated again and again. I have done this deliberately, even though something may be done or put together in exactly the same way as was the toy or doll in the previous chapter. This will enable you to pick up the book, open it to whatever toy you choose, and make it, without having to turn pages to find general directions. You can skip around and make the toys in whatever order pleases you: each set is complete and self-contained.

Please note that even though two toys may look very much alike, they may be finished in a different manner. Some of the toys are sewn together on the wrong side with a back stitch and turned to the right side; others are finished by overcast sewing stitches done from the right side. Therefore, it's important to read and follow the easy finishing instructions for each item carefully.

Always leave a long "tail" of yarn when casting on stitches, adding a new color, or ending your work. This gives you enough yarn to sew your toy together and finish it without cutting, threading, and adding on more.

Use a stitch counter on your knitting needles to keep track of the rows of work, or keep track by marking the row numbers down on paper. Whichever method you choose, this is very important. All of these toys and dolls, because of their size, are measured by rows as you knit, instead of by inches.

To fasten yarn off after sewing edges together, take two or three stitches over and over in the same place; then run the needle through the backs of stitches under completed piece for a little way, come up to the top and carefully clip yarn close to the work.

Unlike most knitted pieces, these toys need not be blocked or pressed. This would only stretch them out of shape. Once they are sewn together and stuffed, they will take shape nicely.

Use only polyester fiberfill for stuffing. Use very small pieces at a time, and push them into place with fingers or the eraser end of a dull pencil. Stuff firmly, but be very careful not to stretch your knitted fabric. Work slowly and carefully, and mold the head, body, and limbs with your fingers as you go along to obtain a pleasing appearance.

If you run out of yarn of one color for a certain animal or really want to use up some scraps, remember that all pieces of the bodies don't have to be the same color. Dogs or cats or even bears or bunnies would be great with legs or arms of different colors. Use your imagination: it's fun, and children love bright colors. The clowns, of course, are ideal for using colors of all kinds. With them, anything goes!

You may not be able to duplicate the exact fabric and trimmings I have used, but please feel free to use whatever you have on hand or personally like. As long as the size (in the case of yarn, the weight) is the same it should work. It will be fun to see what you can create on your own.

Gauge isn't given, because in making toys (unlike in making larger items) it really isn't very important. However, if you know you're a loose knitter, try knitting needles a size smaller than called for. If you're a tight knitter, you may want to use a size larger than called for. Should your sewn-together toy or doll measure larger than the given measurement, remember to add a bit of material when cutting out clothes and try them on your toy before sewing to make sure they will fit properly. Likewise, smaller doll's clothes can be taken in.

I have sewn all clothes directly onto dolls and toys. If you wish to have removable clothes, simply leave openings and sew on snaps or buttons to close—but these should be only on toys for the older children. Moving eyes should be replaced by ones cut from felt or simply embroidered on if the toy is for a very young child.

A Note to Remember: Please be especially careful to remove all pins and needles when work is complete and before giving the toy or doll to a child.

ABBREVIATIONS

K...Knit
P...Purl
beg...beginning
dec...decrease
inc..increase
rem ....remaining
sl ....slip
st(s)...stitch(es)
St st..stockinette stitch
tog ....together
yo..yarn over

THE
TOYS

Country Kids

I call these boy and girl dolls "Country Kids" because of their dress, but I'm sure they would feel right at home in any town or city, too. He wears a striped T-shirt top and blue "denim" overalls, a red bandana around his neck, and a bandana handkerchief tucked in his back pocket. She wears a sweater top, a blue jean skirt, a pinafore apron trimmed with braid that's embroidered with apples, and red-and-white striped knee socks to match her sweater.

They are each 15 inches tall when completed.

To make the boy doll you'll need:

Acrylic yarn of knitting worsted weight:

    1¼ oz light pink (for the head, arms, and legs)

    ½ oz white (for underwear)

    Small amount of red (for socks)

    ½ oz of yarn variegated with bright colors (for T-shirt)

    1½ oz "denim" blue (for overalls)

    Small amount of black (for shoes)

    ½ oz med brown (for hair)

1 red bandana handkerchief (for neckerchief and handkerchief)

Felt: very small piece of brown (for eyes)

Embroidery floss:

    Small amounts each of brown and red (for face)

    A little light brownish-red (for freckles)

    A little black (for nose)

1 pair #4 and 1 pair #6 knitting needles

Stitch holder

Yarn needle

Small amount of red and brown sewing thread

Sewing needle
Polyester fiberfill
Piece of cardboard, 6½ in long

To make the girl doll you'll need:

Acrylic yarn of knitting worsted
    weight:
    1¼ oz light pink (for head, arms,
      and legs)
    ½ oz white (for underwear and
      knee-sock stripes)
    1 oz red (for sweater and knee
      socks)
    1 oz "denim" blue (for skirt)
    Small amount of black (for
      shoes)
    ½ oz yellow (for hair)
White eyelet (for pinafore):
    13 in of 3-inch-wide
    13 in of 1 ¾-inch-wide
    2½ in of 2-inch-wide
1 yd of ½-inch red ribbon (for
    hair)
¾ yd of narrow braid (for pina-
    fore)
Felt: very small piece of brown
    (for eyes)
Embroidery floss:
    Brown and red (for face)
1 pair #4 and 1 pair #6 knitting
    needles
Stitch holder
Yarn needle
Sewing thread to match eyelet,
    braid, eyes, and hair
Sewing needle
Polyester fiberfill
Red-colored pencil
Piece of cardboard, 12 in long

    Both dolls are made in the fol-
lowing way: First, knit the two
pieces alike that are the back and
front of the body and head. Each
has knit-on underwear and shirt
or sweater. Then continue to knit
the head, shaping all as you go
along. The arms and legs are each
knit in one piece, with sleeves,
shoes, and socks knit right on.
Then all the pieces are sewn up,
turned right-side-out, and stuffed.
Hair and features are then added,
the clothes made, and the complete dolls are finished according
to directions.

Make the Country Boy:

Body (make two): Starting at
lower body with #4 needles and
white for underwear, cast on 20
sts. Work in St st for 20 rows.
(The knit side is the right side.)
Next row **To Form Waistline:** K2
tog across—10 sts. Cut white yarn,
then tie on variegated for shirt. P
1 row. *Next row:* K and inc 1 st
in each st across—20 sts. Beg
with P row, work even in St st for
17 rows. *Next row* **To Shape
Shoulders:** Bind off 5 sts at beg

of next 2 rows—10 sts. *Next row:*
P 1 row on right side. Cut variegated yarn, and tie on pink. Beg
with P row, work 4 rows even in
St st for neck. *Next row:* P4, inc
1 st in next st, P5—11 sts. *Next
row* **Head:** K and inc 1 st in each
st across—22 sts. Beg with P row,
work even in St st for 22 rows,
ending with K row. P 1 row, dec
1 st each end—20 sts. *Next row:*
K2 tog across—10 sts. *Next row:*
P2 tog across—5 sts. *Next row:*
K2 tog, K1, K2 tog—3 sts. Cut
yarn, leaving a *long* end. Thread
yarn into yarn needle and pull
through sts as you take them off
the knitting needle. Pull up tight;
fasten yarn, but do not cut. Later
it will be used for sewing together. **Arms** (make two): Beg at
top with variegated yarn for sleeve
and #4 needles, cast on 14 sts.
Work in St st for 10 rows. *Next
row:* P 1 row on right side. Cut
variegated yarn, and tie on pink
for arm. Beg with P row, work
St st for 7 rows. *Next row* (first
dec row): K3, K2 tog, K4, K2 tog,
K3—12 sts. Beg with P row, work
15 rows even in St st. *Next row*
Hand: *K2 tog, K1, repeat from
* across row—8 sts. P 1 row. *Next
row:* *inc 1 st in next st, K1, repeat from * across row—12 sts.
Beg with P row, work 6 rows even
in St st. *Next row:* P2 tog across
row—6 sts. K and bind off. **Legs**
(make two): Starting at top of leg
with #4 needles and pink, cast
on 16 sts. Work even in St st for
12 rows. *Next row:* K4, K2 tog,
K4, K2 tog, K4—14 sts. Beg with
P row, work St st for 11 rows more.
Next row (second dec row): K3,
K2 tog, K4, K2 tog, K3—12 sts.
Beg with P row, work 4 rows even.
Cut pink yarn, and tie on red for
socks. P 2 rows. Beg with P row,

work 5 more rows in St st. *Next row:* (third dec row): K3, K2 tog, K2, K2 tog, K3—10 sts. P 1 row. Cut red yarn, and tie on black for shoe. K 1 row. *Next row:* P across 5 sts, put rem sts onto holder for second side of shoe. *Next row:* Cast on 4 sts at beg of row, then K across row—9 sts. Beg with P row, work 5 rows even in St st. K and bind off. Put sts from holder onto needle, with needle point at center front of leg. Tie on black yarn. P across. K 1 row. *Next row:* Cast on 4 sts at beg of row, then P across all 9 sts. Work 4 rows even in St st. K and bind off.

Finishing:

Body and Head: With right sides held together, using matching yarn and back stitch, sew the two pieces together along the edges, leaving bottom edge open. Turn right side out and stuff firmly, shaping with hands and fingers. Overcast opening closed. **Hair:** Cut a piece of cardboard 6½ in long. Wind brown yarn around this 40 times. Slip all loops carefully off cardboard and lay flat. Cut a piece of yarn 12 in long and use this to tie loosely around all strands, about ⅓ from one end, making a loose, flat bundle that measures about 2½ in across (this tie acts as the "part" in the boy's hair). Carefully pick up bundle and place on head, with "part" to one side as shown. Secure in place by sewing down to head along part. Arrange hair around back and the other side of head, bringing a few strands to front and cutting off for bangs. Sew all loops down around and a little above neckline. Sew

down bangs in place. Cut all loops below sewing and clip ends even around head. Trace and cut out pattern for eyes, then cut eyes from brown felt. Sew in place, with matching thread, using back stitch. Using a double strand of brown floss and outline stitch, embroider heavy eyebrows right above eyes. Use a single strand of red floss and outline stitch to embroider mouth. With a single strand of black, take a few stitches to make a nose. Using brownish-red floss—a single strand—take a few stitches over and over in the same place to make freckles. Repeat in many places around nose and on cheeks to make lots of freckles. **Arms:** Fold arm piece in half—wrong side out—and sew seam as for body and head, leaving top edge open. Turn right-side-out. The easiest way to turn it is to push the bottom inside and keep pushing until it comes out the top, thereby turning to the right side. Stuff firmly, and sew closed by gathering top together. Sew in place on shoulders with seam at underside. At underarms, sew sleeves to body of shirt to hold arm down closer to body. **Legs:** Fold and sew as for arms, sewing shoe sides together across and down around front, across bottom and up the back. Sew back seam, leaving top edge open. Turn by pushing shoe through to top. Stuff and sew closed across top. Sew in place at bottom of body, seam at back, toes to front.

Make the overalls:

First Leg: Beg at waistline edge with #6 needles and denim blue yarn, cast on 22 sts. Work even

in St st for 18 rows. (The knit side is the right side.) *Next row* (inc row): K and inc 1 st at beg and end of row. P 1 row, then repeat inc row once—26 sts. P 1 row. Mark for crotch. Continue for leg. *Next row* (dec row): K and dec 1 st at beg and end of row. P 1 row, K 1 row, P 1 row. *Next row:* Repeat dec row once—22 sts. Beg with P row, work even in St st for 25 rows more. K and bind off. Make second leg in same manner. **Bib:** With same yarn and needles, cast on 14 sts. Row 1 (right side): Sl 1 st knitwise, P 1 st, K to last 2 sts, P 1 st, sl last st knitwise. Row 2: P across. Repeat these 2 rows for a total of 12 rows. K and bind off. **Straps** (make 2): Use same yarn and needles and cast on 30 sts. K 1 row. *Next row:* P and bind off. **Front Left Pocket:** Starting at lower edge, with same needles and yarn, cast on 8 sts. Work even in St st for 6 rows. *Next row:* K and bind off 3 sts at beg of row, K across—5 sts. P 1 row. *Next row:* K2 tog, K3. P 1 row, K 1 row, P 1 row. K and bind off. **Front Right Pocket:** Starting at lower edge, cast on 8 sts. Beg with P row, work St st for 6 rows. *Next row:* P and bind off 3 sts at beg, P across—5 sts. K 1 row. *Next row:* P2 tog, P3. K 1 row, P 1 row, K 1 row. P and bind off. **Back Pockets** (make two): Starting at top edge, cast on 8 sts. Work even in St st for 6 rows. *Next row:* Work across and dec 1 st at beg and end of row. Repeat last row twice—2 sts. Bind off.

Finishing for overalls:

Holding the two leg pieces with right sides together, sew seams for front and back close to edge with a back stitch from waistline to crotch. Refold and sew leg seams in same manner. Turn to right side. Sew cast-on edge of bib in place on front of overalls, using an overcast stitch. Sew on front and back pockets by overcasting in place. Sew one end of straps in place on back of overalls. Put overalls on doll, cross straps at back, bring to front and sew in place to top of bib.

Make the neckerchief and handkerchief:

Cut a piece 8 × 8 in from a red bandana. Hem all edges with narrow hem. Tie around neck. Cut another piece 4 in × 4 in from bandana. Narrowly hem all edges. Fold and put in a back pocket with one corner sticking out to show.

Make the Country Girl:

Body (make two): Starting at lower body, with #4 needles and white for underwear, cast on 20 sts. Work in garter st for 6 rows. Beg with P row, work even in St st for 11 rows. (The knit side is the right side.) *Next row* **To Form Waistline:** P 1 row on right side. *Next row:* P2 tog across—10 sts. *Next row:* P 1 row on right side. Cut white yarn, then tie on red for sweater. P 1 row. *Next row:* K and inc 1 st in each st across—20 sts. Beg with P row, work even in St st for 18 rows (end with K row). **To Shape**

Shoulders: Bind off 5 sts at beg of next 2 rows—10 sts. Work 3 rows in garter st. *Next row:* K4, inc 1 st in next st, K5—11 sts. Cut red yarn, and tie on pink for head. *Next row:* P across. *Next row:* K and inc 1 st in each st across—22 sts. Beg with P row, work even in St st for 22 rows, ending with K row. P 1 row, dec 1 st each end—20 sts. *Next row:* K2 tog across—10 sts. *Next row:* P2 tog across—5 sts. *Next row:* K2 tog, K1, K2 tog—3 sts. Cut yarn, leaving a *long* end. Thread yarn into yarn needle and pull through sts as you take them off the knitting needle. Pull up tight; fasten yarn, but do not cut it. Leave it to be used for sewing together. **Arms** (make two): Beg at top with #4 needles and red for sleeves, cast on 14 sts. Work in garter st for 2 rows. *Next row:* K and inc 1 st in each st across—28 sts. Work 12 rows more of garter st. *Next row* (first dec row): K2 tog across—14 sts. Cut red yarn, and tie on pink for arms. Work St st for 4 rows. *Next row* (second dec row): K3, K2 tog, K4, K2 tog, K3—12 sts. Beg with P row, work 15 rows even in St st. *Next row* **Hand:** *K2 tog, K1, repeat from * across row—8 sts. P 1 row. *Next row:* *inc 1 st in next st, K1, repeat from * across row—12 sts. Beg with P row, work 6 rows even in St st. *Next row:* P2 tog across—6 sts. K and bind off. **Legs** (make two): Starting at top of leg with #4 needles and pink, cast on 16 sts. Work St st for 12 rows. *Next row:* K4, K2 tog, K4, K2 tog, K4—14 sts. Beg with P row, work St st for 3 rows. Cut pink yarn, and tie on red for socks. Work garter st for 4 rows. Tie on white yarn (do not cut red, but carry up side

of work). Work St st for 2 rows. Drop white, pick up red, and work 2 rows in St st. Drop red yarn, and pick up white. *Next row* (second dec row): K3, K2 tog, K4, K2 tog, K3—12 sts. P 1 row with white. Continuing in St st, work additional stripes of 2 rows red, 2 rows white, 2 rows red, and 2 rows white. *Next row* (third dec row): with red, K3, K2 tog, K2, K2 tog, K3—10 sts. With red, P 1 row. Cut red and white yarn, tie on black for shoe. K 1 row. *Next row:* P across 5 sts, put rem sts onto holder for second side of shoe. *Next row:* Cast on 4 sts at beg of row, K across row—9 sts. Beg with P row, work 5 rows even in St st. K and bind off. Put sts from holder onto needle, with needle point at center front of leg. Tie on black yarn. P across. K 1 row. *Next row:* Cast on 4 sts at beg of row; P across all 9 sts. Work 4 rows even in St st. K and bind off.

Finishing:

Body and Head: Hold right sides together, use matching yarn and back stitch to sew the two pieces together close along edges, leaving bottom edge open. Turn to right side and stuff firmly, shaping with hands and fingers as you stuff. Overcast opening closed. **Hair:** Cut a 12 in length of cardboard. Wind yellow yarn around it 40 times. Slip all loops carefully off cardboard and lay flat. Cut a piece of yarn 12 in long and use to tie around all strands at center into a loose flat bundle that measures about 2½ in across. This is the "part" in the hair. Carefully pick up bundle and place on head, with part at center top of head. Secure in place by sewing down to head along part. Arrange hair around sides and back of head. Sew in place around and a little above neckline. Do not cut loops; leave them for curls. **Bangs:** Wind yarn 10 times around a finger. Slip loops carefully off finger and tie together tightly at one end with a piece of yarn. Tuck this end under hairline at forehead and sew in place. Clip ends of tie only; leave loops for curls. Divide long hair in half at back, bring to sides for ponytails, and tie each with red ribbon. Trace and cut out pattern for eyes. Cut eyes from brown felt. Sew in place, with matching thread, using back stitch. Using a double strand of brown floss and outline stitch, embroider heavy eyebrows right above eyes. Use single strand of red floss and outline stitch to embroider mouth and a very small nose. Rub red pencil on cheeks to color. **Arms:** Fold arm piece in half, wrong side out, and sew seam as for body and head, leaving top open. Turn to right side by pushing the hand inside and continuing to push until it comes out the top. Stuff

firmly, and sew closed by gathering top together. Sew in place on shoulders with the seam at underside. At underarms sew sleeves to body of sweater to hold arms down close to body. **Legs:** Fold and sew as for arms, sewing shoe sides together across and down around front, across bottom and up the back. Sew back seam, leaving top open. Turn by pushing shoe through to top, stuff firmly, and sew closed across top. Sew in place at bottom of body, seam at back, toes to front.

Make the skirt:

Front: Beg at waistline edge with #6 needles and blue denim yarn, cast on 20 sts. Work K1, P1 ribbing for 2 rows. Change to St st and work even for 4 rows. (The knit side is the right side.) *Next row* (inc row): K and inc 1 st at beg and end of row. Continue in St st, and repeat inc row on every sixth row thereafter twice more— 26 sts. Work even for 6 rows. Change to garter st and work even for 3 rows. K and bind off. **Back:** Work second piece same as front.

Finishing: Holding right sides together, sew side seams. Turn right side out. Place on doll, pulling up over feet and legs. Sew cast-on edge in place at waistline.

Make the pinafore:

Hem raw edges of 3 × 13 in piece of white eyelet for skirt of pinafore. Lay this flat and place the 2½ in long by 2 in wide piece of eyelet at center top and sew in place for bib. Cut the 13 in long by 1¾ in wide piece into two pieces for the overarm ruffles. Sew one end of each piece in place at each side of bib, tucking end under skirt piece. Try on doll, wrapping skirt around to back and sewing in place on doll, overlapping sides. Bring ruffles over shoulders and down to top of pinafore skirt at back. Sew in place, tucking ends under skirt piece. Cut a length of braid to fit up each side of bib, over each shoulder and down to back waistline. Cut another for around waistline. Sew in place over seams of pinafore. Make a small flat bow of braid and sew in place at back closing.

Eye pattern for Country Kids:

(for boy and girl)

Three Bears

These three teddy bears are all knitted and stuffed in the same way. They are a brown bear, a light (beige)-colored bear, and a panda bear. They all sit about 8 inches high and are made more appealing by the addition of pretty patches of color on their paws, feet, and inner ears. These pieces are cut from print fabric and appliquéd in place. The bears wear pretty ribbon and/or collars around their necks.

By using different colors of yarn and fabric, many cute bears can be made. In fact, the possible combinations are almost endless. Why not make one using your own ideas with whatever you have on hand? I think you'll be pleased.

To make the brown bear you'll need:

Acrylic yarn of knitting worsted weight:
2 oz medium brown
Print fabric: small piece (for appliqués)
⅓ yd blue ribbon
Felt:
7¾ × 1¼ in white (for collar)
Very small pieces of blue, black, and red (for features)
Embroidery floss: small amount of black
1 pair #4 knitting needles
Yarn needle
Sewing thread to match fabric, felt, and ribbon
Sewing needle
Polyester fiberfill (for stuffing)

To make the beige bear you'll need:

Acrylic yarn of knitting worsted weight: 2 oz beige
Print fabric: small pieces (for appliqués)
14 in of 1¼-inch wide white eyelet trim
⅔ yd green ribbon
Felt: very small pieces of green, brown, and red (for features)
Embroidery floss: small amount of brown
1 pair #4 knitting needles
Yarn needle
Sewing thread to match fabric, felt, and eyelet
Sewing needle
Polyester fiberfill

To make the panda bear you'll need:

Acrylic yarn of knitting worsted weight:
1 oz black
1 oz white
Print fabric: small amount (for appliqués)
⅔ yd red velvet ribbon
Felt: small pieces of black and red
2 large moving eyes
Embroidery floss: small amount of black

1 pair #4 knitting needles
Yarn needle
Sewing thread to match fabric, felt, and trims
Sewing needle
Polyester fiberfill for stuffing

The body and head of each bear is knitted in one piece, stuffed and shaped. The legs, ears, and nose are knit separately and sewn on after they have been stuffed and the appliquéd fabric has been added. Then the features are appliquéd and embroidered. Finally, the bears are dressed up with their neckline bows.

Make the brown bear:

Body and Head: Starting at lower edge of body, cast on 40 sts. Work even in St st for 32 rows. (The purl side is the right side). *Next row:* (inc row) *K1, inc 1 st in next st, repeat from * across row— 60 sts. *Next row* **Head:** Beg with P row, work even in St st for 26

7

rows. *Next row:* P2 tog across—30 sts. K and bind off. **Arms** (make two): Cast on 20 sts. Work even in St st for 18 rows. *Next row:* K2 tog across—10 sts. P 1 row. Cut yarn, leaving a long end. Thread yarn into a yarn needle and pull through the sts while taking them off the knitting needle. Pull up tight and fasten yarn, but do not cut yet. Instead, leave it to be used later for sewing arm to body. **Legs** (make two): Cast on 20 sts. Work even for 12 rows. *Next row:* K6, inc 1 st in each of next 8 sts, K6—28 sts. P 1 row. *Next row:* K10, inc 1 st in each of next 8 sts, K 10—36 sts. Beg with P row, work even in St st for 5 rows. *Next row:* K2 tog across—18 sts. P 1 row. K and bind off. **Nose:** Cast on 28 sts. Work St st for 8 rows.

Next row: K2 tog across—14 sts. Cut yarn, leaving a long end, and finish as for arms. **Ears** (make four pieces, two for each ear): Cast on 12 sts. Work even in St st for 6 rows. *Next row:* Work across and dec 1 st at each end of row. Repeat last row 4 times more—2 sts. Cut yarn, leaving long end. Thread into needle and pull through stitches as you take them off the knitting needle. Sew these stitches down firmly to top of ear piece, at the same time rounding the top of the ear. Run in end on wrong side and cut off.

Finishing:

Body and Head: Bring sides of body and head piece together to form a tube with wrong side (knit

side) out. Use yarn needle and matching yarn to overcast edge together. Turn to right side and fold piece flat with seam at center back. Sew closed across top of head. Stuff firmly. Sew closed across bottom edge. **To Form Neckline:** Thread a long length of yarn into yarn needle. Working on inc row, take a few stitches to secure yarn at back seam. Wrap yarn around bear twice, pulling hard to pull piece in, forming neck. Holding firmly, return to where yarn was first secured and secure again with several stiches. Run end in under work and cut off. **Arms:** Thread yarn that was pulled through last stitches of arms into needle. Pull up tight, bringing sides together and forming a tube (wrong side out). Fasten securely. Take a few stitches to close lower end completely. Using matching yarn, overcast seam where sides were brought together. Turn to right side. Stuff. Fold flat at upper edge with seam to one side, and sew closed across top.   **Legs:** Fold leg piece flat (wrong side out) with inc part (toe) to one side and edges together at other side. Overcast seam across bottom and up side. Turn to right side. Stuff, pushing out inc part to form toe. Run a matching yarn around top, gather to close and secure.   **Ears:** Place two ear pieces together (wrong side out) and overcast edges together, working around curved edges only, *twice* to make it firm. Do not overcast bottom edge. Do not stuff. Turn right side out. Trace and cut out patterns for fabric patches. Cut patches from fabric. Using matching thread, and turning in all raw edges, appliqué fabric patches in place on inner ears, inside paws, and bottoms of feet as shown. Using yarn, sew ears, arms, and legs to body and head piece. Place ears on sides of head at the ends of top seam. Place arms at sides of body, facing forward, appliqués on inner side. Place legs on lower front body with toes facing forward and up, so that the bear can sit up.   **Face:** Thread yarn that was pulled through last stitches of nose into yarn needle. Pull up tightly to gather and fasten, taking a few stitches to completely close end of nose. On wrong side overcast seam formed by pulling sides of piece together.

Turn right side out. Stuff firmly. Sew in place on face, with seam at underside. Using patterns, cut eyes from blue felt, nose tip from black felt, and tongue from red felt. Using matching thread and back stitch sew all in place. With six strands of black floss, embroider lines down nose and along mouth as shown. Using pattern, cut collar from white felt. Place around neck. Make bow from ribbon, trim and sew in place on collar front.

Make the beige bear:

Knit and assemble using the directions for the brown bear, through completion of finishing of nose. Using same patterns, cut eyes from green felt, nose tip from brown felt and tongue from red felt. Sew in place with matching thread. With brown floss, embroider line down nose and along mouth as shown in the photograph. Hem ends of white eyelet. Gather to fit around bear's neck and sew in place, for collar. Place ribbon around neck, over collar, and tie in bow at front.

Make the panda bear:

Body and Head: Starting at lower edge of body with white yarn, cast on 40 sts. Work even in St st for 22 rows. (The knit side is the right side.) Cut white yarn, and tie on black. Work even in St st for 10

rows. *Next row:* (inc row) *K1, inc 1 st in next st, repeat from * across row—60 sts. Cut black yarn, and tie on white again. **Head:** Continuing to work with white and beg with P row, work even in St st for 26 rows. *Next row:* P2 tog across—30 sts. K and bind off. Following directions for brown bear, use black to knit arms, legs, and ears. Use white to knit nose. Using yarns to match panda color, follow brown bear directions for finishing, *EXCEPT* that all seams are sewn on the *right* (knit) side of bear, and the bear is stuffed without turning.

Using patterns, cut the eye patches and the nose tip from black felt, and cut the tongue from red felt. Sew in place with matching thread. Sew moving eyes on top of eye patches. Be sure to sew on very securely, or, better yet, if toy is for a young child who could pull them off, either add a patch of white felt on top of black for eyes or embroider them on. Embroider line down nose and along mouth with black floss. Cut red ribbon to fit around neck of bear. Cut additional pieces to make a flat bow and sew all in place under chin.

Patterns for Three Bears

Ear patch

Paw patch

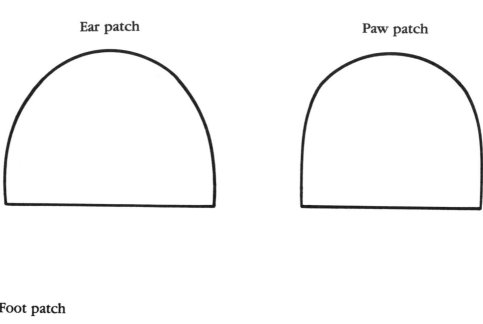

Foot patch

Eye

Nose

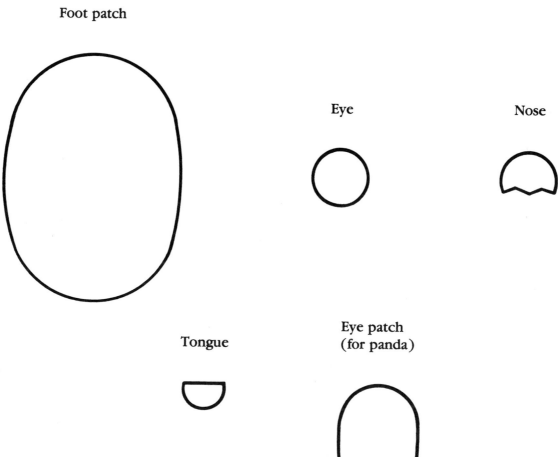

Tongue

Eye patch
(for panda)

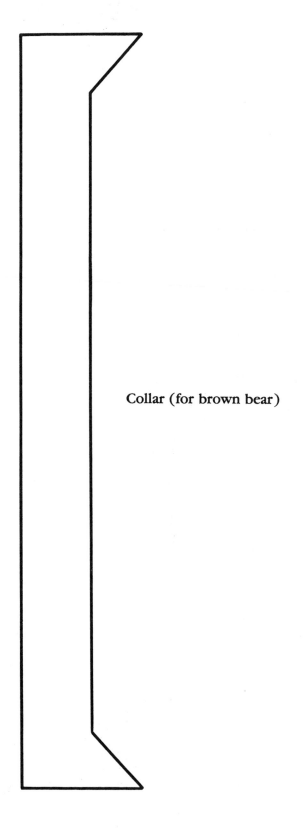

Collar (for brown bear)

Sailor Boy and Girl

This little boy and girl are all dressed up in their old-fashioned sailor suits, which have distinctive flowing collars tied in front with red ribbon. He wears a hat with his and she has a ribbon in her hair. They are 7½ inches tall.

To make each sailor boy or girl you'll need:

Acrylic yarn of knitting worsted weight:
  ½ oz white

½ oz pink
½ oz yellow
½ oz dark blue
Very small amount of black
Very small amount of red
½ yd narrow white braid
1 yd narrow red grosgrain ribbon

Felt: small piece of dark blue (for collar)
Embroidery floss: medium blue and red
1 pair #4 knitting needles
Stitch holder
Yarn needle

Sewing thread: yellow, white, and red
Sewing needle
Polyester fiberfill
Red-colored pencil
Piece of cardboard, 4½-in-long (for boy)
Piece of cardboard, 5½-in-long (for girl)

The body and head of each is made in one piece and sewn together with a center back seam. The arms and legs are knit separately and added.

Make the Sailor Boy:

Body: Starting at the lower edge of underpants, using white, cast on 18 sts. Work in garter st for 2 rows. Change to St st and work 7 rows even. *Next row:* K 1 row on wrong side to indicate waistline. Continuing with white for blouse, work even in St st for 10 rows. You are now at the neckline. Cut white yarn, and tie on pink. *Next row* **Head:** *K2, inc 1 st in next st, repeat from * across—24 sts. Beg with P row, work even in St st for 9 rows. *Next row:* K2 tog across—12 sts. *Next row:* P2 tog across—6 sts. Complete as follows: Cut yarn, leaving a long end for sewing. Thread yarn into needle and pull through sts as you take them off knitting needle. **Arms:** Starting at upper arm for puff sleeve of blouse, using white, cast on 12 sts. Work in St st for 5 rows. Cut white, tie on red and use to K2 tog across row on wrong side—6 sts. Cut red, tie on pink and work even in St st for 10 rows.

Next row: K3 tog twice—2 sts. Complete as for top of head. **Legs:** Starting at top of leg with pink, cast on 8 sts. Work even in St st for 6 rows. Cut pink, tie on red and work 2 rows of garter st. Cut red, tie on white and work even in St st for 6 rows. Cut white, tie on black for **Shoe:** K across 4 sts. Put remaining 4 sts on st holder for second half of shoe. *Next row* (working on first side only): Cast on 2 sts at beg of row, P across row—6 sts. K 1 row, P 1 row. *Next row:* K and bind off. **Second Half of Shoe:** Put sts from holder onto left-hand needle, with point at middle of leg. Using black, cast 2 sts onto right hand needle then K across 4 sts on left needle—6 sts. *Next row:* P across. K 1 row. P1 row. *Next row:* K and bind off.

Make pants:

(Make two, one each for front and back): Starting at waistline with dark blue, cast on 12 sts. K 1 row, P 1 row. (The knit side is the right side.) *Next row* (inc row): inc 1 st in first st, K to within last 2 sts, inc 1 st in next st, K1—14 sts. Beg with P row, work 3 rows St st. *Next row:* Repeat inc row—16 sts. Beg with P row, work 5 rows even. **Divide Work For Legs:** *Next row:* K 8 sts, place remaining 8 sts on holder to be worked later for second leg. *First leg:* Beg with P row, work 3 rows even. K and bind off. *Second leg:* Put sts from holder onto left-hand needle, with point at center of work. Tie on yarn and K across. Complete as for first leg.

Make hat:

Using dark blue, cast on 40 sts. **Brim:** Work even in St st for 4 rows (the knit side is the right side). *Next row* **Crown:** K2, K2 tog across—30 sts. P 1 row. *Next row:* K2, K2 tog across to last 2 sts, end K2—23 sts. P 1 row. *Next row:* K2 tog across to last st, end K1—12 sts. P 1 row. *Next row:* K2 tog across—6 sts. Cut yarn, leaving a long end for sewing seam. Thread yarn into yarn needle and pull through sts as you take them off knitting needle.

Finishing:

Assembling Body: Thread yarn that was pulled through last stitches of head into yarn needle, pull up tightly, bringing sides together and forming a right-side-out tube. Fasten securely at top of head, and, using matching yarns, seam sides together. Stuff firmly. Fold piece flat at bottom edge with seam at center back. Using white yarn, sew closed across bottom edge. **To Form Neckline:** Thread a long length of white yarn into yarn needle. Working on last row of white on body at neckline, take a few stitches at back seam to secure yarn. Wrap yarn around doll twice pulling hard to pull piece in to form neck. Hold firmly, return to where yarn was first secured, and take several stitches to secure again. Cut yarn. **Arms:** Using matching yarns, sew hand end of arm closed and sew seam as for body and head. Stuff arm, stuffing white sleeve part very firmly to puff out. Using white yarn in needle, run yarn in and out of work around upper edge of sleeve and pull up to puff. Fasten. Sew arms onto sides of body with seam at underside of arm. **To Form Wrist and Hand:** Wrap pink yarn around arm about ½ in up from end in same manner as for neckline. **Legs and Shoes:** Using matching yarns, sew seam around shoe and up back of sock and leg. Stuff firmly. Fold flat across top with seam at back and sew closed. Sew in place at bottom of body. **Hair:** Wind yellow yarn around a 4½ in piece of cardboard 15 to 20 times for desired thickness. Slip off, carefully laying bundle flat. Tie loosely at center with another strand of yellow yarn, spreading bundle out to measure 1¼ in across. Put in place on head, with tie in yarn along top of head for "part" in hair. Spread evenly over head. With matching thread, sew in place, using back stitch along part. Sew ends down around head at about ear level. Cut five or six short strands of yarn, fold and tuck folds under front hairline for bangs. Sew in place under hairline and across forehead. Cut all loops and trim to desired length. **Face:** Use six strands of medium blue floss and satin stitch to make eyes. Use one strand of red floss to embroider a very small nose in satin stitch and a mouth in outline stitch. **Pants:** Using matching yarn, with right sides held together, sew seams at sides and inner legs with overcast stitch. Turn. Pull pants onto boy and sew in place at waistline. **Collar:** Trace and cut out pattern and use to cut a sailor collar from blue felt. With white thread, sew a piece of white braid around outside edge of collar. Place around boy's neck,

with points meeting at center front of chest. Sew in place, taking a few stitches through front of doll to secure. Cut a 4½ in piece of red grosgrain ribbon, make a single knot at center, and sew knot in place on front of collar, ends hanging down. Trim. **Hat:** Pull up and secure last stitches of hat for crown. Bring sides of piece together and overcast seam on wrong side, allowing first four or five rows worked to roll back to form brim. Purl side will show on right side. Turn hat to right side. Cut a 12 in piece of ribbon and, using matching thread, sew in place around crown of hat just inside of brim, allowing two ends of about 3 in each to hang down from center back at seam for streamers. Place hat on head and sew securely in place.

Make the Sailor Girl:

Knit body and head, arms and legs exactly as for boy.

Make skirt:

Starting at top edge and using blue, cast on 24 sts. *Row 1* (wrong side): *K2, P1, repeat from * across row. *Row 2* (right side): *K1, P2, repeat from * across row. Repeat last 2 rows once. *Next row* (first inc row): *K1, inc 1 st in next st, P1, repeat from * across row—32 sts. *Next row:* *K1, P3, repeat from * across row. *Next row:* *K3, P1, repeat from * across row. Repeat last 2 rows once, then repeat the first one of them once more. *Next row* (second

inc row): *K1, inc 1 st in next st, K1, P1, repeat from * across row—40 sts. *Next row:* *K1, P4 repeat from * across row. *Next row:* *K4, P1, repeat from * across row. Repeat last 2 rows once. Bind off in ribbing as established, on right side of work.

Finishing:

Finish and assemble body, arms and legs in same manner as for boy. **Hair:** Wind yellow yarn around a 5½ in piece of cardboard 20 times. Slip off carefully, laying bundle flat. Tie loosely around at center with yellow yarn, spreading bundle out to measure 1¼ in wide. Place on head with tie in yarn along top of head for "part" in hair, but do not sew down yet. Wind yarn around cardboard again 5 times. Slip off carefully, holding in a bundle. Slip all loops at one end of bundle under hair at hairline on forehead. Sew down to head. Now sew all hair in place on head, using back stitch along part and around neckline. Pull group of yarn that was sewn under at forehead up and over hair toward back of head. Tie in a bundle on top of head using matching thread or yarn. Allow to hang down over back of head. Wind yarn over one finger, slip off and sew in place at sides of face for extra curls. **Face:** Using six strands of medium blue floss, embroider eyes in satin stitch. Use one strand of red floss to embroider a very small nose in satin stitch and a mouth in outline stitch. To color cheeks, rub lightly with a red pencil. **Skirt:** Bring sides of skirt pieces together, right side out and whip stitch along edge for seam. Put in place on girl by pulling up over feet and legs to waistline. With seam at center back, sew in place, pulling tight as you sew to "nip in" waist. **Collar:** Trace and cut out pattern and use to cut a sailor collar from blue felt. With white thread, sew a piece of white braid around outside edge of collar. Place around girl's neck, with points meeting at center front of chest. Sew in place, taking a few stitches through front of doll to secure. Cut a 4½ in piece of red grosgrain ribbon. Make a single knot at center, and sew knot in place on front of collar, ends hanging down. Trim. **Ribbon:** Cut a piece of red grosgrain ribbon 12 in long. Tie in small bow at center. Sew bow to top of head, over strands brought back from forehead, allowing long ends (3 in or so) to hang down over back of head.

Pattern for Sailor Boy and Girl:

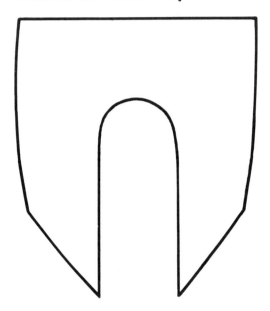

Sailor collar (for boy and girl)

Three Little Kittens and Mother Cat

Unlike the three little kittens in the nursery rhyme, these three kittens have already found their mittens and each one has them tied securely to a cord hung around its neck. The two little girl kittens are dressed in gingham checked skirts and the little boy kitten wears pants made of felt. Mother cat also wears a checked gingham outfit and a smile because she now has such good little kittens. The kittens are 6 inches tall and mother cat is 11½ inches tall.

To make each kitten you'll need:

Acrylic yarn of knitting worsted weight:
  1 oz white (for first girl kitten)
  1 oz gray (for second girl kitten)
  1 oz brown variegated (for boy kitten)
  Very small amount of red and orange (for girls' mitten cords)
  Very small amount of yellow (for boy's mitten cord)
Small-checked gingham fabric:
  1 piece 10 in × 2 in of blue (for first kitten)
  1 piece 10 in × 2 in of pink (for second kitten)
Narrow Bias Binding:
  6 in piece of blue
  6 in piece of pink
Felt: small pieces of red, orange, yellow and green
Embroidery floss: small amounts of green, red, and black
1 pair #4 knitting needles
1 crochet hook size 0
Yarn needle

Sewing thread to match felt and gingham
Sewing needle
Polyester fiberfill

To make the mother cat you'll need:

Acrylic yarn of knitting worsted weight:
  2½ oz beige variegated
Red gingham fabric in medium-sized check:
  1 piece 22 in × 3½ in
  1 piece 2 in × 3 in
Red bias binding: 24 in long
Felt: Small pieces of medium green, dark green, and brown
Embroidery floss: small amount of brown
Small red and green purchased motif for front of dress
1 pair #4 knitting needles
Yarn needle
Sewing thread to match felt and gingham
Sewing needle
Polyester fiberfill

The body and head of each kitten and cat is made in one piece and sewn together with a center back seam. The arms and legs are made separately and added.

Make the first girl kitten:

Body: Starting at lower edge of body with white yarn, cast on 20 sts. Work even in St st for 16 rows. *Next row:* (inc row) *K1, inc 1 st in next st, repeat from * across row—30 sts. **Head:** Beg with a P row. Working on these 30 sts, work even in St st for 13 rows. *Next row:* K2 tog across row—15 sts. P and bind off. **Arms:** (make two) Cast on 10 sts. Work even in St st for 8 rows. Complete as follows: Cut yarn, leaving a long end for finishing. Thread end into yarn needle and pull through sts as you take them off knitting needle. **Legs:** (make two) Cast on 10 sts. Work even in St st for 12 rows. Complete as for arms. **Ears:** (make two) Cast on 7 sts. Work even in St st for 7 rows. P

and bind off.   **Tail:** Cast on 12 sts. Work even in St st for 4 rows. K and bind off.

Finishing:

Bring sides of body and head piece together to form a tube with knit side (right side) out. Sew seam, using matching yarn and overcast stitch. Fold piece flat with seam down center back. Sew piece closed across top of head. Stuff firmly. Sew closed across bottom edge.   **To Form Neckline:** Thread a long length of matching yarn into yarn needle. Working on inc row, take a few stitches to secure yarn at back seam. Wrap yarn around kitten twice, pulling hard to pull piece in to form neck. Hold firmly and return to where yarn was secured, and secure again with several stitches. Clip yarn after hiding end in work.   **Arms:** Thread yarn that was pulled through last stitches of arm into yarn needle. Pull up tightly, bringing sides together and forming tube knit side out. Fasten securely. Take a few stitches to close outer end completely. Sew seam where sides were brought together. Stuff firmly. To finish upper end, run yarn in and out around edge to gather. Pull up to close and fasten. Sew onto kitten at side of body with seam at underside.   **Legs:** Thread yarn that was pulled through last stitches of leg into needle. Finish this end as for outer end of arms. Sew seam. Stuff firmly. To finish top of leg, fold and sew straight across top with seam at center back or on inner side of leg. Sew in place on kitten at lower edge of body.   **Ears:** Fold each ear piece into a triangle, knit side out. Using matching yarn, sew open edges together by overcasting along edges. Overcast along these edges once more to make a firm edge. Sew folded edge of ears to kitten's head at each end of head seam, curving outer edges ahead and up a bit to form rounded ears. Sew both back and front of ears to secure in place. **Tail:** Thread yarn left from binding off into needle. Run yarn in and out through one *short* side of work to gather purl side out. Pull up tightly and secure, forming piece into a rolled shape, and closing end. Overcast edges of cast on and bound off rows together. Do not stuff for kittens; stuff lightly for mother cat. Piece will naturally curl a little. Sew open end closed and sew in place on back of kitten, with tail curling to one side. **Faces For All Kittens:** Using several strands of green embroidery floss, embroider eyes in satin stitch. Use several strands of black to make satin stitch nose and to work mouth in outline stitch. Take a few small satin stitches, with red floss, just above mouth outline for tongue. To make whiskers, use a single strand of black floss. Take three long straight stitches out from each side of nose to side of face. Bring needle back, out of sight, under face each time to nose. Securely fasten off thread.

Dress the first kitten:

Use blue gingham piece to make a skirt. Sew a small hem on one long side and the two short sides of piece. Gather the other long side to fit the 6 in piece of blue bias binding and sew in place. Wrap skirt around kitten and sew in place at waistline with ends folded over in back. Bring tail to outside from under fold. Using red yarn, crochet a chain 9 in long. To make two mittens, use pattern to cut four red mitten pieces from red felt. Using matching thread, sew two pieces together to make each mitten. Sew one mitten to each end of crocheted cord. Tie cord loosely around neck with mittens hanging in front.

Make the second (girl) kitten:

Use gray yarn to knit. Finish and dress in same manner as first kitten, using pink gingham and bias tape to make skirt. Crochet cord from orange yarn and make mittens from orange felt.

Make the third (boy) kitten:

Use brown variegated yarn to knit and finish as for first kitten. Using pattern for pants, cut two pieces from green felt. Sew the two pieces together at front from top down to crotch. Repeat for back seam, leaving an opening for tail to come through. Fold flat with seams at center front and back. Sew leg seams, matching other seams at crotch. Turn to right side. Stitch a false fly front with matching thread. Pull onto kitten, pulling tail out through back opening. Take a few stitches through pants and body at back seam and fly front to hold in place. Crochet cord from yellow yarn and make mittens from yellow felt.

Make the mother cat:

Body: Starting at lower edge of body, cast on 40 sts. Work even in St st for 32 rows. *Next row:* (inc row) *K1, inc 1 st in next st, repeat from * across row—60 sts. **Head:** Beg with P row work even in St st on these 60 sts for 26 rows. *Next row:* P2 tog across—30 sts. K and bind off. **Arms** (make two): Cast on 20 sts. Work even in St st for 14 rows. *Next row:* K2 tog across—10 sts. P 1 row. Complete as follows: Cut yarn, leaving a long end for sewing. Thread yarn into needle and pull through sts as you take them off the knitting needle. **Legs** (make two): Cast on 20 sts. Work even in St st for 22 rows. *Next row:* K2 tog across—10 sts. P 1 row. Complete as for arms. **Ears** (make two): Cast on 14 sts. Work even in St st for 15 rows. P and bind off. **Tail:** Cast on 24 sts. Work even in St st for 8 rows. K and bind off, leaving end for finishing.

Finishing:

Follow directions for finishing and assembling kittens through completion of tail. Remember to stuff the tail a little for the mother cat. **Face for the mother cat:** Using pattern, cut two round eye pieces from medium green felt and two inner eye pieces from dark green felt. Sew inner eye piece onto round eye piece with points extending up and down center, as shown. Sew eye in place on face using matching thread and back stitch. Using pattern, cut nose from brown felt and sew in place as for eyes. Using brown floss, embroider mouth in outline stitch. To make whiskers, use two strands of brown floss. Take three long straight stitches out from each side of nose to side of face. Bring needle back after each stitch, out of sight, under face, to nose. Securely fasten off thread. Fine lines of outline stitch may be used instead, if you wish.

To dress the mother cat:

To make dress, hem one long side and two short sides of larger piece of gingham for skirt. Cut a piece of bias binding 11½ in long for skirt band. Gather the other long side of skirt piece to fit band and sew in place. Make a very narrow hem on all four sides of the smaller gingham piece for bib to go onto skirt. Sew bib to top of skirt band at center front. Sew motif in place on bib. For straps, measure two pieces of bias binding that will be long enough to fit from top of bib over shoulders, cross in back, and come down again to skirt band in back. Sew one end of each to each side of bib at top front, tucking ends under. Place dress on cat, wrapping skirt to back and straps over shoulders. Sew band and straps down in back (tucking raw ends under), taking a few stitches through cat to hold in place. Bring tail to outside from under skirt.

Patterns for Three Little Kittens and Mother Cat

Mitten

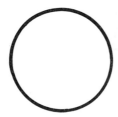

Pants (for boy)

(place left edge on fold)

Outer eye (for mother)

Inner eye (for mother)

Nose (for mother)

Puss in Boots

*This cat wears boots and carries a bag like the one in the story "Puss in Boots."
He also wears a colorful belt and jaunty hat with a pretty feather in it. He is
12½ inches tall.*

To make Puss in Boots you'll need:

Acrylic yarn of knitting worsted
weight: 2½ oz gray
1 yd of red patterned, 1-in-wide
braid
1 yd narrow white braid
Felt:
Small piece of red
Very small pieces of light and
dark green
9 × 12 in piece of black
1 small "brass" buckle
1 large red feather (I cut mine
from a feather duster)
Embroidery floss: small amount
of black
1 pair #4 knitting needles
Yarn needle
Sewing thread to match all felt
and both braids
Sewing needle
Polyester fiberfill

Note: To make this toy safe for
a young child, both the feather
and the belt buckle could be cut
from felt (patterns are given), or
else the belt can be used without
a buckle.

The body and head are knit in
one piece and sewn up with a
center back seam. The arms and
legs are knit separately and sewn
on.

Make Puss in Boots:

Body: Starting at lower edge of
body, cast on 40 sts. Work even
in St st for 32 rows. *Next row
(inc row):* *K1, inc 1 st in next
st, repeat from * across row—60
sts. **Head:** Beg with P row, work

even in St st on these 60 sts for 26 rows. *Next row:* P2 tog across—30 sts. K and bind off. **Arms** (make two): Cast on 20 sts. Work even in St st for 14 rows. *Next row:* K2 tog across—10 sts. P 1 row. Complete as follows: Cut yarn, leaving long end for sewing. Thread yarn into needle and pull through sts as you take them off knitting needle. **Legs** (make two): Cast on 20 sts. Work even in St st for 22 rows. *Next row* (dec row for instep): K2 tog* K1, K2 tog, repeat from * across row—13 sts. **Foot:** Beg with P row, work even in St st for 7 rows. *Next row:* K2 tog across to last st, end K1—7 sts. P 1 row. Complete as for arms. **Ears** (make two): Cast on 14 sts. Work even in St st for 15 rows. P and bind off. **Tail:** Cast on 24 sts. Work even in St st for 8 rows. K and bind off, leaving long end for finishing.

Finishing:

Bring sides of body and head piece together to form a tube, with right side (knit side) out. Overcast these sides together, using matching yarn. Fold piece flat with seam up and down center back. Sew piece closed across top of head. Stuff firmly. Sew closed across bottom edge. **To Form Neckline:** Thread a long length of matching yarn into yarn needle. Working on inc row, take a few stitches to secure yarn at back seam. Wrap yarn around cat twice, pulling hard to pull piece in to form neck. Hold firmly and return to where yarn was secured and secure again with several stitches. Cut yarn and hide end in work. **Arms:** Thread yarn

that was pulled through last stitches of arm into yarn needle. Pull up tightly, bringing sides together and forming tube (knit side out). Fasten securely. Take a few stitches to close this outer end completely. Overcast seam where sides were brought together. Stuff firmly. To finish upper end, run yarn in and out around edge to gather. Pull to close and fasten. Sew onto cat at side of body with seam at underside. **Legs:** Thread yarn that was pulled through last stitches of leg into needle. Finish this end as for outer end of arms. Sew seam. Stuff firmly. To finish upper end, fold end flat with seam at back side and sew together straight across top. To form foot more firmly at instep, sew back and forth with matching yarn on front of leg along dec row from foot to leg, pulling up tightly to bring foot forward and hold it in place. Sew legs in place on cat at lower edge of body, feet pointing to front. **Ears:** Fold ear piece into a triangle (knit side out). With matching yarn, overcast open edges together. Overcast along these edges once again to make a firm edge. Sew folded edge to cat's head at each end of head seam, curving outer edge ahead and up a bit to form rounded ear. Sew both back and front of ear to secure. **Tail:** Thread yarn left from binding off into needle. Run yarn in and out through one short side of piece to gather. Pull up tightly and secure, forming piece into rolled shape and closing end with purl side out for right side. Overcast edges of cast on and bound off rows together. Stuff lightly. Piece will naturally curl a little. Sew open end closed, and sew in place on back of cat with

tail curling to one side. **Face:** Using patterns, cut eye pieces from felt. Cut two round outer pieces from light green and two inner pieces from dark green. Using matching thread, sew each inner eye piece to round outer piece with points extending up and down through center of eye. Sew eyes in place on face using back stitch. Cut nose from black felt and sew in place. Use six strands of floss to embroider mouth in outline stitch. To make whiskers, use two strands of floss in needle and take three long straight stitches from each side of nose to cheeks, as shown. Take a very small stitch to secure on cheek, if you wish, but do not cut thread. Run needle, out of sight, under face and back to side of nose, and fasten off. Whiskers may instead be made of very thin outline stitch, if you wish.

Make belt:

Measure and cut piece of 1 in braid long enough to fit around cat's middle plus an inch or so for overlap. Place "brass" buckle or one cut from felt on braid a little from one end. Put around cat, with buckle at center front. Fold in raw edge and sew in place, taking a few stitches through cat to secure.

Make boots:

Using pattern, cut four boot pieces from black felt. For each boot sew two pieces together, taking a ¼ in seam. Turn to right side and place on cat.

Make hat:

Using pattern, cut hat from black felt. Fold piece in half on fold line. Sew outer edges together, from top to bottom, taking a ¼ in seam. Turn to right side. Cut a piece of narrow white braid long enough to fit around hat ½ in up from lower edge, plus enough to tie ends. Knot ends together and trim. Sew onto hat, with knot at seam.

Cut real feather or one made of felt to desired length and tuck end under knot. Sew in place on hat. Place hat over one ear and sew securely to head at several points.

Make bag:

Using pattern, cut two pieces from red felt. Turn down ½ in at top edge on each piece to form casing. Sew in place. Sew the two pieces together up to the casings, leaving casings open. Turn to right side. Cut two 12 in pieces of narrow white braid. Thread one piece through entire casing, ends coming out to right edge of bag. Tie a knot in each end, then tie ends together. Repeat with second piece of braid, ends coming out to left edge of bag. Tie as before. Pull braid at each end to close bag and hang ties over cat's arm.

Patterns for Puss in Boots

Hat

Boots

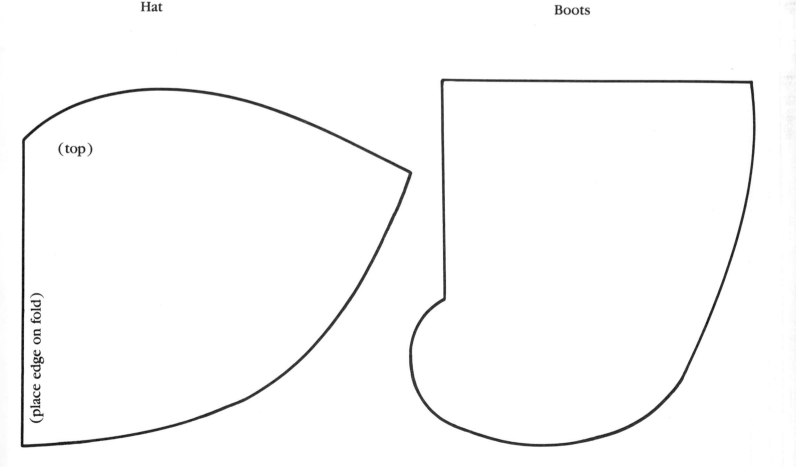

(top)

(place edge on fold)

Feather

Bag

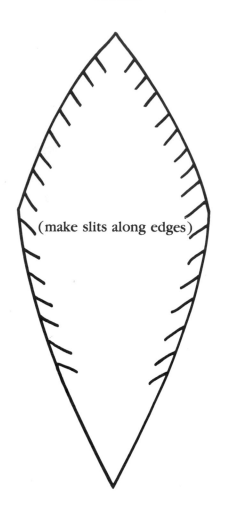

(make slits along edges)

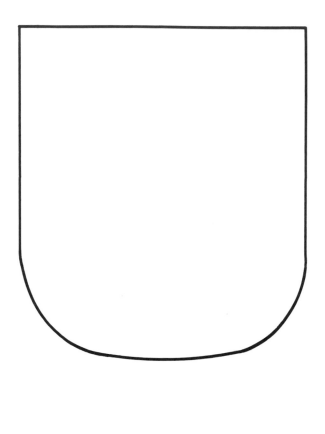

Buckle

Nose

Inner eye

Outer eye

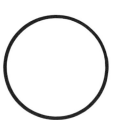

Eight Little Dolls

These little dolls are all from the pages of some of our favorite nursery rhymes and stories. There's Hansel and Gretel in flower-trimmed outfits, Little Boy Blue all dressed up in blue, and Red Riding Hood in a red, hooded cape. There's Alice in Wonderland with her long blonde hair and Mistress Mary, holding lots of flowers from her garden. The last two are based on Grimm's Snow-White and Rose-Red, but I call my dolls Rose White and Rose Red.

All of the dolls are approximately 7 inches tall and are made in the same general manner. The addition of the hair and features and lots of different trims give each doll "personality plus."

On all stockinette stitch pieces, the knit side is the right side.

HANSEL AND GRETEL

To make Hansel you'll need:

Acrylic yarn of knitting worsted weight:
- ½ oz pink
- ½ oz medium green
- ½ oz beige
- ½ oz white
- ½ oz yellow (for hair)
- Small amount of black (for shoes)

12 in narrow green grosgrain ribbon

Felt: very small pieces of red, orange, and yellow

Embroidery floss: small amounts of red and medium blue

1 pair #4 knitting needles

Stitch holder

Yarn needle

Sewing thread to match ribbon, felt, and hair

Sewing needle

Polyester fiberfill

4½ in piece of cardboard

To make Gretel you'll need:

Acrylic yarn of knitting worsted weight:
- ½ oz pink
- ½ oz medium green
- ½ oz light green
- ½ oz white
- ½ oz yellow (for hair)
- Small amount of black (for shoes)

14 in of ½-inch flower-print trim

Embroidery floss: small amounts of red and medium blue

1 pair #4 knitting needles

Stitch holder

Yarn needle

Sewing thread to match trim and hair

Sewing needle

Polyester fiberfill

Red-colored pencil

9 in long piece of cardboard

The body and head are knit in one piece and formed with a seam down the center back. The arms and legs are knit separately and sewn in place. Shoes and stockings for each doll are knit right onto the legs, and all of the blouses and shirts are knit as part of the body piece. Skirts and pants are knit separately and sewn in place.

Make Hansel:

Body: Starting at lower edge, with white for underpants, cast on 18 sts. Work even in St st for 8 rows (the knit side is the right side). Cut white, tie on beige for shirt and work in St st for 12 rows. Cut beige, tie on pink. *Next row* **Head:** *K2 inc 1 st in next st, repeat from * across row—24 sts. Beg with P row work even in St st for 9 rows. *Next row:* K2 tog across—12 sts. *Next row:* P2 tog across—6 sts. Complete as follows: Cut yarn leaving long end for sewing. Thread yarn into yarn needle and pull through stitches as you take them off knitting needle. **Arms:** Starting at upper arm with beige for sleeve, cast on

6 sts. Work even in St st for 5 rows. Cut beige, tie on green and use to K 1 row on wrong side for stripe. Cut green, tie on pink for arm and work St st for 10 rows. *Next row:* K3 tog twice—2 sts. Complete as for top of head. **Legs:** Starting at top of leg with pink, cast on 8 sts. Work even in St st for 6 rows. Cut pink, tie on green for stripe and use to work 2 rows in garter st. Cut green, then tie on beige for **Sock.** Work even in St st for 6 rows. Cut beige, tie on black and use to make **Shoes.** K across 4 sts. Put remaining 4 sts onto st holder for second half of shoe. *Next row* (working on first side only): cast on 2 sts at beg of row, P across row—6 sts. K 1 row, P 1 row. *Next row:* K and bind off. **Second half of Shoe:** Put sts from holder onto left-hand needle, with point at middle of leg. Using black, cast 2 sts onto right-hand needle, then K across 4 sts on left needle—

6 sts. *Next row:* P across. K 1 row. P 1 row. *Next row:* K and bind off.

Make pants:

(Make two alike, one each for front and back): Starting at waistline with green, cast on 12 sts. K 1 row, P 1 row (the knit side is right side). *Next row* (inc row): inc 1 st in first st, K to within last 2 sts, inc 1 st in next st, K1—14 sts. Beg with P row, work 3 rows St st. *Next row:* Repeat inc row—16 sts. Beg with P row, work 5 rows even. *Next row* **Divide Work For Legs:** K8 sts, place remaining 8 sts on holder to be worked later for second leg. **First leg:** Beg with P row, work 3 rows even. K and bind off. **Second leg:** Put sts from holder onto left-hand needles, with point at center of work, tie on yarn and K across. Complete as for first leg.

Finishing:

Assembling Body and Dressing: Thread yarn that was pulled through last stitches of head into yarn needle, pull up tightly, bringing sides together (right side out) to form a tube. Fasten securely, and, using matching yarns, whip stitch sides together. Stuff firmly. Fold piece so it is flat across bottom edge and seam is at center back. Using matching yarn, sew closed across bottom edge. **To Form Neckline:** Thread a long length of yarn to match top (shirt or blouse) into yarn needle. Working on last row of body at neckline, take a few stitches at back seam to secure yarn. Wrap yarn around doll twice, pulling hard to pull piece in to form neck. Hold firmly, return to where yarn was first secured, and take several stitches to secure again. Cut yarn. **Arms:** Using matching yarns, sew hand end of arm closed, and sew seam as for body and head. Stuff firmly. Run yarn in and out of work around upper edge of sleeve. Pull up and fasten. Sew arms onto sides of body with seam at underside of arm. **To Form Wrist and Hand:** Wrap pink yarn around arm about ½ in up from end in same manner as for neckline. **Legs and Shoes:** Using matching yarns, sew seam around shoe and up back of sock and leg. Stuff firmly. Fold flat across top with seam at back and toes front. Sew closed. Sew in place on body. **Hair:** Wind yellow yarn around a 4½ in piece of cardboard, 15 to 20 times (according to how thick you want it). Slip off, carefully laying the bundle flat. Tie loosely around the bundle at center with another strand of yellow yarn, spreading bundle out so it measures 1¼ in wide. This tie acts as a "part." Put yarn in place on head, with part along center of head. Spread hair evenly over head. With matching

thread, sew in place, using back stitch along part. Sew ends down around head at about ear level. Cut five or six short strands of yarn, fold and tuck folds under front hairline for bangs. Sew in place under hairline and across forehead. Cut all loops and trim to desired length. **Face:** Using six strands of medium blue floss, embroider eyes in satin stitch. Using one strand of red floss, embroider a very small nose in satin stitch and a mouth in outline stitch. **Pants:** Using matching yarn, holding right sides together, sew seams at sides and inner legs with overcast stitch. Turn right-side-out. Pull pants onto Hansel, and sew in place at waistline, pulling in waistline as you sew. **Straps:** Measure and cut 2 pieces of ribbon to fit over shoulders from front waistline to back waistline. Cut a piece of ribbon to fit across chest between straps and another piece of the same

length to go across the back. Sew together, place on doll and sew in place. Cut two very small hearts from red felt. Cut a very small flower from orange felt and a center for the flower from yellow felt. Using matching thread, sew hearts in place on front. Place one where each end of cross ribbon meets straps. Sew center to flower and sew flower in place at middle of front cross ribbon.

Make Gretel:

Body: Starting at lower edge, with white for underpants, cast on 18 sts. Work garter st for 2 rows. Change to St st and work 6 rows even. Cut white, tie on light green for blouse and, changing to garter st, K even for 12 rows. Cut light green, tie on pink.

To make head:

Next row: *K2, inc 1 st in next st, repeat from * across row—24 sts. Beg with P row work, even in St st for 9 rows. *Next row:* K2 tog across. Next row P2 tog across—6 sts. *Complete as follows:* Cut yarn, leaving long end for sewing. Thread yarn into yarn needle and pull through sts as you take them off knitting needle. **Arms:** Starting at upper arm, with light green for sleeve, cast on 12 sts. Work in garter st for 5 rows. *Next row:* K2 tog across—6 sts. Cut light green, tie on pink for arm and work in St st for 10 rows. *Next row:* K3 tog twice—2 sts. Complete as for top of head. **Legs:** Starting at top of leg with pink, cast on 8 sts. Work even in St st for 6 rows. Cut pink, tie on light green for stripe and use to work

2 rows in garter st. Cut green, tie on white for sock and use to work even in St st for 6 rows. Cut white, and tie on black. **Shoes:** K across 4 sts. Put remaining 4 sts onto st holder for second half of shoe. *Next row—* working on first side only: Cast on 2 sts at beg of row, P across row—6 sts. K 1 row, P 1 row. *Next row:* K and bind off. **Second Half of Shoe:** Put sts from holder onto left-hand needle, with point at middle of leg. Using black, cast 2 sts onto right-hand needle, then K across 4 sts on left needle— 6 sts. *Next row:* P across. K 1 row. P 1 row. *Next row:* K and bind off.

Knit skirt:

With medium green, starting at waistline edge, cast on 24 sts. Work 2 rows even in St st. (The knit side is the right side.) *Next row:* *K2, inc 1 st in next st, repeat from * across row—32 sts. Beg with P row, work even in St st for 11 rows. *Next row:* K and bind off.

Finishing:

Assembling Body and Dressing: Finish body and head piece in same manner as for Hansel. Finish arms and legs as for Hansel, stuffing sleeves firmly to make them "puff out," and sew all in place on doll. **Hair:** Wind yellow yarn around a 9 in long piece of cardboard 12 times. Slip off carefully, laying bundle flat. With another strand of yarn, tie loosely around at center, spreading bun-

dle out so it measures 1¼ in wide. Place on head, with tying yarn along center top of head to form "part" in hair. Spread evenly over head. With matching thread, sew in place, using back stitch along part. Sew down around head at about ear level. Divide ends into two groups. Bring one group to each side of head and form into a braid on each side. Tie ends tightly with medium green yarn bows. Clip loops and trim ends even. Cut five or six short strands of yarn for bangs. Fold and tuck ends evenly under front hairline. Sew in place. Do not cut the loops: leave for curls. **Face:** Make face in same manner and colors as for Hansel. Rub cheeks lightly with red pencil to give them color. **Skirt:** Bring side edges of skirt piece together (wrong side out) and overcast together. Turn to right side. Measure and cut piece of trim to fit around lower edge of skirt. Using matching thread, sew in place. Pull skirt up over legs onto doll and sew in place at waistline. For straps, measure two pieces of trim to fit over shoulders from front waistline to back waistline. Sew in place.

LITTLE BOY BLUE

To make Little Boy Blue you'll need:

Acrylic yarn of knitting worsted weight:
½ oz pink
½ oz white
½ oz medium blue
½ oz dark blue

½ oz red-orange (for hair)
Small amount of black (for shoes)
5 in narrow blue velvet ribbon
Embroidery floss: small amounts of red, medium blue, and orange
1 pair #4 knitting needles
Stitch holder
Yarn needle
Sewing threads to match ribbon and hair
Sewing needle
Polyester fiberfill
4½-in-long piece of cardboard

Make Little Boy Blue:

Body: Knit the body and head piece, arms and legs in the same manner as for the Hansel doll, using medium blue yarn for socks and shirt in place of beige, and dark blue for pants in place of green. Make the stripes on shirt sleeves and tops of socks using white in place of green. When knitting shirt on body piece (with medium blue), work for 10 rows instead of 12. Knit the pants the same as for Hansel, using dark blue yarn.

Finishing:

Body: Finish and assemble body and head piece, arms and legs as for Hansel. **Hair:** Using red-orange yarn, wind and make hair in same manner as for Hansel. Place on head with "part" to left side. For bangs, some of the strands can be brought forward over right side of the forehead or extra loops can be added. Using matching thread, sew all in place and clip ends evenly. **Face:** Embroider face in same manner as for Hansel. Using a single strand of orange floss and satin stitch, make a few freckles around nose and over cheeks. **Pants:** Sew together, place and sew on doll as for Hansel.

Using narrow velvet ribbon, make a "bow tie," and, with matching thread, sew in place under chin.

LITTLE RED RIDING HOOD

To make Little Red Riding Hood you'll need:

Acrylic yarn of knitting worsted
   weight:
   ½ oz white
   ½ oz pink
   ½ oz red
   ½ oz black (for hair and shoes)
   ½ oz dark red (for cape)
12 in narrow (about ½-inch)
   white braid
Embroidery floss: small amounts
   of red and medium green
1 pair each of #4 and #6 knitting
   needles
Crochet hook size G or 6
Stitch holder
Yarn needle
Sewing thread to match trim and
   hair
Sewing needle
Polyester fiberfill
5 in-long piece of cardboard

Make Little Red Riding Hood:

Doll: With #4 needles, knit the body and head piece, the arms, and the legs in the same manner as for the Gretel doll, using red for the blouse in place of green. On legs, no contrasting stripe is used on socks: instead, use white for the 2 rows of garter st, then continue with white for the 6 rows of St st, down to the shoe. Knit the skirt as for Gretel, using red yarn and #4 needles. The first 2 rows can be worked in ribbing of K1, P1 instead of St st if you wish.

Make cape with hood:

Using #6 needles and dark red yarn, starting at top of head for hood, cast on 21 sts. *1st row:* K1, P1 across row to last st, and K1. Repeat this row 17 times—a total of 18 rows. *Next row:* Eyelet row: K1 * yo, K2 tog, repeat from * across row. *Next row:* K across, working all yo's as K sts—21 sts. *Next row:* *K and inc 1 st in next st, K2, repeat from * across row—28 sts. *Next row:* K1, P1 across row, inc 1 st in last st—29 sts. Continue for cape: Work in pattern of K1, P1 across to last st, end K1, as for hood, for 18 rows. Change to garter st and work for 8 rows. K and bind off. Fold piece double and sew tog across top of hood. With crochet hook, make a chain 10 in long. Thread through eyelet row.

Finishing:

Body: Finish and sew together body and head piece, arms and legs as for the Hansel and Gretel dolls. **Hair:** Using black yarn, make hair in same manner as for Hansel doll, winding around a 5 in cardboard 15 times. Sew to head in same manner, but do not cut or trim loops at ends or bangs. Instead, leave them for curls. **Face:** Make face same as for Hansel and Gretel dolls, using red for nose and mouth and green instead of blue for eyes. **Skirt:** Trim and sew skirt tog and onto doll as for Gretel, omitting straps. Measure, cut and sew a piece of trim around neckline to match trim on skirt. Place hooded cape on doll and tie under chin.

ALICE IN WONDERLAND

To make Alice in Wonderland you'll need:

Acrylic yarn of knitting worsted
   weight:

   ½ oz white
   ½ oz pink
   ½ oz medium blue
   ½ oz yellow (for hair)
   Small amount of black (for
      shoes)

White eyelet
   1 piece 1¾-inch, 6 in long
   2 pieces 1-inch, 4 in long
14 in narrow pink rick-rack
Embroidery floss: small amounts
   of red and medium blue
1 pair #4 knitting needles
Stitch holder
Yarn needle
Sewing thread to match hair, eyelet, and rick-rack
Sewing needle
Polyester fiberfill
Red-colored pencil
8 in-long piece of cardboard

Make Alice:

Body: Make the body and head piece and the arms in the same manner as for the Gretel doll, using blue yarn for the blouse and sleeves and working these in St st instead of garter st. When working blouse, work for 10 rows instead of 12. When working sleeves, work 5 rows for sleeve. *Next row:* P2 tog across, then change to pink for arm and finish as for Gretel. **Legs** are made differently, with striped stockings, as follows: With white, cast on 8 sts. Work 2 rows of St st. Drop white; do not cut, but leave at side of work. Tie on blue and use to work 2 rows of St st. Drop blue, pick up white, and work 2 rows of St st. Continue in this manner alternating colors every 2 rows and weaving them up side of work for a total of 7 stripes, ending with a white stripe. Cut both blue and white, tie on black and use to knit shoe as for Gretel.

Make skirt:

Using blue, make skirt in the same manner as for Gretel.

Finishing:

Body: Finish and assemble body and head piece, arms and legs as for Hansel and Gretel. Take extra care to match stripes of stockings. **Hair:** Make hair in same manner as for Gretel winding around an 8 in cardboard 15 times. Sew to head in same way, along "part" in center, and sew down around back of head, a little above ear level. Omit bangs. Clip all ends to hang straight, long, and even over shoulders and down back. **Face:** Work face in same manner and colors as for Hansel and Gretel. Rub cheeks lightly with red pencil for color. **Skirt:** Sew skirt together and onto doll as for Gretel. Hem raw edges on each piece of eyelet trim. Measure, cut, and sew a piece of rick-rack along one edge of each piece. Place larger piece around waistline for apron effect. Put two smaller pieces over shoulders for straps, tucking in ends at waistline, under the larger piece. Sew all in place on doll.

MISTRESS MARY

To make Mistress Mary you'll need:

Acrylic yarn of knitting worsted weight:
 ½ oz pink
 ½ oz white
 ½ oz yellow
 ½ oz light brown (for hair)
 Small amount of black (for shoes)
Embroidery floss: small amounts of red and brown
About 6½ in narrow flower-printed braid
1 bunch* very small artificial flowers
1 pair #4 knitting needles
5 in-long piece of cardboard
Stitch holder
Yarn needle
Sewing thread to match trim and hair
Sewing needle
Polyester fiberfill

*If the doll is for a very small child, omit bouquet and use only a few flowers sewn very securely to hair.

Make Mistress Mary:

Body: Work body and head piece and arms in the same manner as for Gretel, using yellow for the blouse and sleeves in place of green. Work the legs in the same manner, omitting stripe—instead use white for the 2 rows of garter st and continue with white for the 6 rows of St st for socks, down to shoes.

To make skirt:

Using yellow, knit skirt exactly as for Gretel.

Finishing:

Body: Finish and assemble all pieces as for the Hansel and Gretel dolls. **Hair:** Make hair in same manner as for Gretel, winding around a 5 in cardboard 15 times. Sew to head in same way along "part" and around head at ear level. Omit bangs. Do not cut or trim loops at ends: instead, leave them for curls. **Face:** Make face the same as for Gretel, using red for mouth and nose and brown instead of blue for eyes. **Skirt:** Trim and sew skirt together and onto doll as for Gretel, omitting straps. **Adding flowers:** Take a few flowers from bunch and sew to hair at each side of face and at center back of head. Bring arms together at front of doll and sew together. Place remaining flowers in a bunch inside of arms. Sew stems to hands to hold in place.

ROSE RED AND ROSE WHITE

These "sister dolls" are so much alike I'll list the things needed and directions for making them together.

To make these sisters you'll need:

Acrylic yarn of knitting worsted weight:
  1 oz red (for Rose Red)
  1 oz white (for Rose White)
  Small amount of white (for Rose Red's panties and socks)
  ½ oz pink for each doll
  ½ oz. brown (for Rose Red's hair)
  ½ oz yellow (for Rose White's hair)
  Small amount of brown (for shoes)
½ in flower printed braid trim
  2 ft each of red and green print (for Rose Red)
  2 ft each of blue and green print (for Rose White)
Eyelet trim:
  1 piece 1½ in wide—6 in long of white (for Rose Red)
  1 piece 1½ in wide—12 in long of light green (for Rose White)
Embroidery floss: small amounts of red and blue for each doll
1 pair #4 and 1 pair #6 knitting needles
Crochet hook size G or 6
Stitch holder
Yarn needle
Thread to match trim, eyelet and hair
Sewing needle
Polyester fiberfill
9 in long piece of cardboard

Make Rose Red or Rose White:

Body: Knit the body and head piece the same as for Gretel, using #4 needles and red yarn for Rose Red, or white for Rose White in place of light green for blouse. Work blouse in St st instead of garter st for 10 rows instead of 12. **Note:** Since both the panties and blouse on Rose White are knit with white, you might want to P1 row on right side of work at waistline (just before blouse) to indicate it. **Arms:** Work arms in same manner as for Gretel, using red or white in place of green, working 5 rows in St st. *Next row:* P2 tog across, change to pink, and finish as for Gretel. **Legs:** Knit in same manner as for Gretel, working the socks entirely in white, including garter st stripe (no contrasting stripe), and the shoes in brown instead of black.

Make clothes:

Skirt: Starting at waistline edge and using #6 needles, red for Rose Red or white for Rose White, cast on 24 sts. K 1 row. P 1 row. *Next row:* *K1, K and inc 1 st in next st, repeat from * across row—36 sts. Beg with P row work even in St st for 15 rows. K and bind off.
Bonnet: Starting at face edge, with #6 needles and red or white to match doll, cast on 20 sts. Work in St st for 5 rows. At beg of next 2 rows, bind off 7 sts. Working on rem 6 sts, for back piece of hat and beg with P row, work even in St st for 8 rows. P and bind off.

Finishing:

Body: Finish and sew together body and head piece, arms and legs as for Hansel and Gretel dolls. **Hair:** Make hair in same manner as for Hansel, using brown yarn for Rose Red and yellow yarn for Rose White and winding around a 9 in cardboard 15 times. Sew to head in same way, omitting bangs and leaving ends in long loops to hang down back for curls. **Face:** Make the same as for Hansel and Gretel. **Skirt:** Trim and sew skirt together and onto doll as for Gretel, omitting straps on Rose Red. **To Finish Rose Red:** Hem raw edges on white eyelet piece and gather top edge to fit at waistline as an apron. Sew in place. Cut and sew a piece of braid trim to fit entirely around waistline. Sew in place on top of upper edge of apron. **To Finish Rose White:** Make an apron of green eyelet that wraps completely around doll's skirt, and add braid trim at waistline as for Rose Red. Also cut and add shoulder straps made from braid, tucking ends under waistline braid and sew in place. **Bonnet:** Sew first two bound off edges to sides of back piece. Crochet two ties, each 5 in long, and sew to sides of bonnet. On Rose Red's bonnet sew a piece of trim along face edge. For Rose White's make a bow of trim and sew to center top front edge of bonnet. Place on head and tie bow at one side of chin.

Betty and Billy Bunny

Here are two bunnies that are soft and cuddly. I call the girl bunny Betty and the boy Billy. Each is 14 inches tall and wears a knit-on sweater with trim appliquéd on. They make a cuddly pair.

To make Betty Bunny you'll need:

Acrylic yarn of knitting worsted weight:
  1 oz white
  ½ oz light pink
  ½ oz dark pink
2 large flower appliqués—white and pink colored
Felt: small pieces of black, blue, and purple
Embroidery floss: small amount of black
1 pair of #6 knitting needles
Stitch holder
Yarn holder
Sewing thread to match appliqué and felt (or contrast, if you wish)
Polyester fiberfill

To make Billy Bunny you'll need:

Acrylic yarn of knitted worsted weight:
  1 oz light brown
  ½ oz medium blue
  ½ oz light blue
Felt: small pieces of black, blue, and enough red for nose and appliquéd letter on front of sweater
Embroidery floss: small amount of red

1 pair #6 knitting needles
Stitch holder
Yarn needle
Sewing thread to match (or contrast with) felt
Sewing needle
Polyester fiberfill

The body (including sweater) and head of each bunny is made in one piece with a center back seam. Arms are made separately and sewn on. They are knitted us-

ing #6 needles to make them soft. Perhaps, however, you would rather have a bit firmer toy. If so, knit them using #4 needles and following same directions. Remember that the completed Bunny will be a bit smaller—but just as much fun to snuggle.

Make Betty Bunny:

First Leg: Using white yarn, cast on 18 sts. Work even in St st for

33

22 rows. Cut yarn. Put sts onto st holder. (K side is right side). **Second Leg:** Work same as first leg until 22 rows are completed. *Next row:* K across 18 sts on needle, slip the 18 sts from st holder onto left needle and K across these, putting all 36 sts onto right needle. Continuing to work on these 36 sts for **Body,** beg with P row work even in St st for 3 rows. Cut white, tie on dark pink for sweater stripe and use to work 6 rows in garter st. Cut dark pink, tie on light pink for body of sweater, change to St st and work even for 14 rows. Cut light pink, tie on dark pink again, change to garter st and work 4 rows. Cut dark pink, tie on white for **Head** and work even in St st for 20 rows. **Divide For Ears:** Next row K and bind off 2 sts, then K across until there are 14 sts on right needle. Place these sts on st holder, to be worked later, for second ear. Bind off next 4 sts, K across to end—16 sts. *Next row* **First Ear:** P and bind off first 2 sts, P across to end—14 sts. Work even on these 14 sts in St st for 20 rows. *Next row* (Dec for tip): *K2 tog, K1, repeat from * across to last 2 sts, end K2 tog—9 sts. *Next row:* P2 tog across to last st, end P1— 5 sts. Complete as follows: Cut yarn, leaving long end for sewing. Thread yarn into needle and pull through sts as you take them off knitting needle. **Second Ear:** Place sts from holder—right side facing—onto right needle with point toward center of head. Tie on white yarn and beg with P row, work St st for 21 rows. Dec for tip and complete as for first ear. **Arms:** Starting at outer end, with white, cast on 18 sts. Work even

in St st for 6 rows. Cut white, tie on dark pink for stripe on sweater sleeve and use to work 4 rows in garter st. Cut dark pink, tie on light pink for sleeve and work 7 rows in St st. Cut yarn and complete as for ears.

Finishing:

Body: Bring sides of body piece together at center back—wrong side out—to form a tube shape. Pin sweater and head part together, matching colors, but do not sew yet. **For Legs:** Thread matching yarn into needle and run in and out around bottom edge of leg to gather. Pull up tight and fasten. Sew bottom closed and then sew leg seam up to crotch. Repeat for second leg, joining legs at crotch. **For Ears:** Thread yarn that was pulled through last sts of ear into needle. Pull up tightly, fasten securely and then sew inside seam of ear down to top of head. Repeat for second ear. Sew small seam closed across top of head. Sew back seam of head, leaving the rest of body (sweater) open. Turn. Stuff all parts. Using matching yarn, sew opening closed. **To Form Neckline:** Thread a long length of yarn, of color to match head, into yarn needle. Working just above last garter stitch row of sweater, take a few stitches to secure yarn at back seam. Wrap yarn around bunny twice, pulling hard to pull piece in to form neck. Return to where yarn was secured and secure again with several stitches. **Define Ears:** Using matching yarn pull around base of ears right next

to head and secure in same manner as for neck. **Finish Arms:** Bring sides of arm piece together—wrong side out. With matching yarn, close and finish outer end in same manner as for legs. Sew seam of arm and sleeve with matching yarns. Turn. Stuff. Thread yarn that was pulled through last stitches of sleeve into needle, pull up tightly and fasten securely. Sew onto side of bunny's sweater just below neckline garter stitch stripe, with seam at underside of arm. **Tail:** Using yarn to match leg and body color, make a 1½ in pom-pom. Sew to back at top of legs. **Face:** Using pattern, cut two eye pieces of black felt and two eye pieces of blue felt for each bunny. Cut one nose piece of purple felt. Using either matching or contrasting thread and back stitch, sew eyes in place, with blue eye piece underneath and extending a little above black piece. Sew nose in place with matching or contrasting thread. Using black embroidery floss, work 2 long stitches into a wide V shape for mouth. Sew flower appliqués to front of sweater, one above the other, with a few stitches of matching thread.

Make Billy Bunny:

Body: Using light brown yarn in place of white, knit legs and body same as for Betty Bunny. Cut light brown and tie on medium blue and use to work sweater part as follows: Continuing on 36 sts, work 6 rows in garter st. Drop medium blue; do not cut. Tie on light blue. Change to St st and work 2 rows. Drop light blue, pick up medium blue and work 2 rows even. Alternating colors as established and carrying color not in use up side of work, work an additional 2 rows light blue, 2 rows medium blue, 2 rows light blue, 2 rows medium blue and 2 rows light blue for a total of 14 rows of St st. Cut light blue. Change to garter st and work 4 rows with medium blue. Cut medium blue, tie on light brown and K to complete head and ears as for Betty Bunny. **Arms:** Starting at outer end, with light brown,

cast on 18 sts. Work even in St st for 6 rows. Cut light brown, tie on medium blue and use to work 4 rows of garter st. Do not cut. Tie on light blue and use to work 2 rows in St st. Continuing to alternate colors as for sweater body, work 2 more rows medium blue, 2 rows light blue and 2 rows me-

dium blue for a total of 8 rows in St st. Cut yarn and complete as for ears.

Finishing:

Body: Finish, sew together and make tail the same as for Betty Bunny. Make face the same way using red felt instead of purple for nose and use red floss to make mouth. Use pattern to cut letter from red felt and appliqué to front of sweater with matching thread.

Patterns for Bunnies

Letter (for Billy's sweater)

Eyes

Nose

Goldilocks and the Three Bears

These old favorites are all dressed up to go walking. Goldlilocks is 7 inches tall and wears knit-on clothes except for her skirt, which is made of fabric. Father Bear is 8½ inches tall, Mother Bear is 7½ inches tall and Baby Bear is 6 inches tall. With the addition of their features, Goldilocks's long blonde hair, and "dressing up" the bears, they become very lovable.

GOLDILOCKS

To make Goldilocks you'll need:

Acrylic yarn of knitting worsted weight:
   ½ oz light pink
   ½ oz white
   ½ oz rose
   ½ oz yellow (for hair)
   Small amount of brown (for shoes)
2¼ × 11 in piece of small-flower-print fabric
5½ in of narrow bias tape to match fabric
Embroidery floss: small amount of red and brown
1 pair # 4 knitting needles
Stitch holder
Yarn needle
Thread to match fabric and hair
Sewing needle
Polyester fiberfill
9 in long piece of cardboard

All are made in the same general manner. The body and head are made in one piece with a center back seam. The arms and legs are made separately and sewn on. Goldilocks, Mother Bear and Baby Bear are knit using #4 needles, but #6 needles are used to make Father Bear.

Make Goldilocks:

Body: Starting at lower edge of panties, with white yarn, cast on 18 sts. Work in garter st for 12 rows. Cut white, tie on rose for blouse and work in garter st for 12 rows (up to neckline). Cut rose, tie on light pink. *Next row* **Head:** (inc row) *K2, inc 1 st in next st, repeat from * across row— 24 sts. Change to St st and beg with a P row work even for 9 rows (the knitted side is the right side). *Next row:* K2 tog across. *Next row:* P2 tog across—6 sts. **To complete:** Cut yarn, leaving a long end for sewing. Thread yarn into yarn needle and pull through sts as you take them off knitting needle. **Arm:** Starting at top of sleeve, with rose yarn, cast on 12

sts. Work even in garter st for 5 rows. *Next row:* K2 tog across row—6 sts. Cut rose, tie on light pink for arm and work even in St st for 10 rows. *Next row:* K3 tog twice—2 sts. Complete as for body and head piece. **Legs:** Using light pink and starting at top of leg, cast on 8 sts. Work even in St st for 6 rows. Cut light pink, tie on rose and work 2 rows in garter st. Change to St st and work even for 6 rows. Cut rose, tie on brown and use to make **Shoes:** K across 4 sts. Put rem 4 sts on st holder for second half of shoe. *Next row* (Working on first side only): cast on 2 sts at beg of row, P across row—6 sts. K 1 row, P 1 row. *Next row:* K and bind off. **Second Half of Shoe:** Put sts from holder onto left-hand needle, with point at middle of leg. Using brown, cast 2 sts onto right-hand needle then knit across 4 sts on

left needle—6 sts. *Next row:* P across. K 1 row. P 1 row. K and bind off.

Finishing:

Body and Head: Thread yarn that was pulled through last 6 stitches of head into needle. Pull up tightly, bringing sides together and forming tube (right side out). Fasten securely at top of head and using matching yarns, sew back seam. Stuff firmly. Fold piece flat at bottom edge, so the seam is up and down center back. Using matching yarn, sew closed across bottom edge. **To Form Neckline:** Thread a long length of rose yarn into yarn needle. Working on last row of rose on blouse at neckline, take a few stitches to secure yarn at back seam. Wrap yarn around doll twice, pulling hard to pull piece in to form neck. Hold firmly and return to where yarn was se-

cured. Secure again with several stitches. **Arms:** Using matching yarns, close hand end of arms and sew seam as for body and head. Stuff firmly. Using rose yarn in needle, run yarn in and out of work around upper edge of sleeve and pull up to "puff" sleeve. Fasten yarn. Sew arms onto sides of sweater body with seams at undersides of arms. To form wrist and hand, wrap light pink yarn around arm about ½ in up from end in same manner as for neck. **Legs and Shoes:** Using matching yarns, sew seam around shoe and up back of sock and leg. Stuff firmly. Fold top together with seam at back and sew closed. Sew in place at bottom of body. **Hair:** Wind yellow yarn around a 9 in cardboard 15 times. Slip off carefully, laying bundle flat. Do not cut looped ends. Tie bundle together loosely at center, with another strand of yellow yarn,

spreading out so it measures 1¼ in across. Put in place on head with tying yarn along center top of head as "part" in hair. Spread evenly over head and, with matching thread, sew in place using back stitch along part. Pull hair over the shoulders, toward back, and sew in place with back stitch just above neckline. Looped ends can hang down back as curls. Wind yellow yarn around a finger 4 or 5 times to make curly bangs. Slip off carefully and sew in place on forehead with matching thread. Wrap a piece of rose yarn around hair at neckline, along stitching line. Tie into a bow, on top of hair, at back of neck. **Face:** Use six strands of brown embroidery floss and satin stitch to make eyes. Use red floss and straight stitches to make a very small nose and a mouth. **Skirt:** Using matching thread, hem one long side and the two short ends of fabric. Gather and sew the other long side onto bias tape for waistband. Wrap skirt around doll at waistline, overlapping at back. Sew in place.

THE BEARS

To make Father Bear you'll need:

Acrylic yarn of knitting worsted weight:
　1 oz dark brown
　¼ oz light brown
9 in of ½-inch black flat braid or bias tape (for straps)
14 in of decorative braid, 1 in wide, in bright colors (for belt and bow tie)
Felt: small piece of black (for pants)
1 in "brass" buckle
Embroidery floss: small amount of black
1 pair # 6 knitting needles
Yarn needle
Sewing thread to match felt and trim
Sewing needle
Polyester fiberfill

To make Mother Bear you'll need:

Acrylic yarn of knitting worsted weight:
　¾ oz dark brown
　¼ oz light brown
　¼ oz red (for shawl)
13 in × 2½ in piece of striped fabric (for skirt)
6½ in bias tape to match skirt fabric
18 in. narrow blue ribbon
Embroidery floss: small amount of black
1 pair #4 knitting needles

Yarn needle
Sewing thread to match skirt and ribbon
Sewing needle
Polyester fiberfill

To make Baby Bear you'll need:

Acrylic yarn of knitting worsted weight:
　½ oz dark brown
　¼ oz light brown
6 in of ½-in red striped bias tape (for straps)
Felt: small piece of red (for pants)
2 very small white buttons
Embroidery floss: small amount of black
1 pair #4 knitting needles
Yarn needle
Sewing thread to match felt and buttons
Sewing needle
Polyester fiberfill

Make Father Bear:

Body: Starting at lower edge of body, with dark brown, cast on 22 sts. Work in St st for 18 rows. (The knit side is the right side.) *Next row* (inc row): *K1, inc 1 st in next st, repeat from * across— 33 sts. *Next row* **Head:** P 1 row. Work even in St st for 14 rows. *Next row:* K2 tog across to last st, end K1—17 sts. P and bind off. **Arms:** Starting at upper end, with dark brown, cast on 12 sts. Work even in St st for 8 rows. Cut dark brown, tie on light brown and use to K 1 row, P 1 row. *Next row:* K2 tog across—6 sts. **Complete as Follows:** Cut yarn, leaving long end for sewing. Thread yarn into yarn needle and pull through sts as you take them off knitting needle. **Legs:** Starting at upper

end, with dark brown, cast on 12 sts. Work even in St st for 12 rows. Cut dark brown, tie on light brown and use to K 1 row, P 1 row. *Next row:* K2 tog across—6 sts. Complete as for arms. **Ears:** (make four pieces— two for each ear): Starting at lower edge using light brown, cast on 8 sts. Work even in St st for 4 rows. *Next Row:* K and dec 1 st each end of row—6 sts. *Next row:* P and dec 1 st each end of next row—4 sts. *Next row:* K2 tog twice. Cut yarn, leaving long end. Thread into needle and pull through rem 2 sts as you take them off needle. Sew these 2 sts firmly down to top of ear piece, thereby rounding the top of the piece. Run in end on wrong side of piece to hide, and clip off. **Nose:** Using light brown yarn, cast on 16 sts. Work even in St st for 4 rows. Complete as for arms and legs, pulling yarn through sts.

Finishing:

Body and Head: Bring sides of body and head piece together to form a tube (right side out). With matching yarn, overcast edges together. Fold piece flat with seam at center back. Sew piece closed across top of head. Stuff firmly. Sew closed across bottom edge. **To Form Neckline:** Thread a long length of matching yarn into yarn needle. Working on inc row, take a few stitches to secure yarn at back seam. Wrap yarn around bear twice, pulling hard to pull piece in to form neck. Hold firmly and return to where yarn was secured and secure again with several stitches. **Arms:** Thread yarn that was pulled through last stitches of arm piece into needle. Pull up tightly, bringing sides together and forming a tube (right side out). Fasten securely. Take a few stitches to close lower end completely. Using matching yarns, sew seam where sides were brought together. Stuff firmly. With dark brown yarn in needle, run yarn in and out around upper edge to gather. Pull up tight and fasten. Sew closed. Sew onto bear at side of body with seam at underside of arm. **Legs:** Thread yarn that was pulled through last stitches of leg into needle. Finish this end as for lower end of arms. Sew seam with matching yarns. Stuff firmly. Fold top of leg flat with seam at back or inside of leg. With matching yarn, sew closed; then sew in place on lower edge of body. **Ears:** Place two ear pieces (for each ear) together with right sides out. Overcast edges together, working around curved edges twice to make firm. Sew one ear in place at each end of seam on head. **Nose:** Thread yarn that was pulled through last stitches of nose into yarn needle. Pull up tightly to gather and fasten. Take a few stitches to completely close end of nose. Sew seam formed by pulling sides of piece together. Stuff firmly. Sew in place on face with seam at underside of nose. **Face:** Using six strands of embroidery floss, work eyes and tip of nose in many satin stitches.

Make clothes:

Pants: Using pattern for pants, cut two pieces alike from black felt. Sew the two pieces together for front seam from top down to crotch. Sew back seam together

in same way. Fold flat, seams at front and back. Sew leg seams, matching the other seams at crotch. Turn right side out. Put on bear. Turn up cuffs. Measure and cut black braid or bias binding to fit over shoulders for straps and sew in place to top of pants. Measure a piece of colored braid to fit around bear's waist—plus a little for overlap. Place braid around top of pants, with buckle slipped onto one end. Sew in place with buckle at center front and overlap sewn down to fit. Buckle may be omitted or made of felt. **Tie:** Cut a 4 in piece of colored braid trim and fold double, overlapping ends on underside. With matching thread, gather tightly at center front and secure in bow shape. Sew in place under "chin."

Make Mother Bear:

Body: Using #4 knitting needles, instead of #6, follow the exact same directions for knitting and finishing Father Bear, then dress as follows:

Make clothes:

Skirt: Make a narrow hem on one long side and the two short sides of skirt piece. Gather and sew the other long side to bias tape for skirt band. Wrap around bear at "waistline" with a fold over at back. Sew together and onto bear to hold in place. Measure and cut two pieces of blue ribbon to fit over shoulders—plus a little extra, for straps. Sew in place, tucking ends under skirt band. **Hair Ribbon:** Tie a small piece of ribbon into a bow and sew to top

of head between ears.

Knit shawl:

Using #4 needles and red yarn and beg at top edge, cast on 32 sts. *Row 1*— * wrap yarn around needle, P2 tog, repeat from * across row. Repeat this one row for pattern for a total of 1½ in. P and bind off loosely. Thread a long piece of red yarn into yarn needle and run it in and out along cast on edge of shawl. Cut yarn leaving ends long enough for ties on shawl. Place shawl around Mother Bear's shoulders. Pull ties to gather in a little and tie in a bow at front.

Make Baby Bear:

Body: Using dark brown and starting at lower edge, cast on 18 sts. Work even in St st for 14 rows. (The knit side is the right side.) *Next row:* (inc row) *K1, inc 1 st in next st, repeat from * across— 27 sts. Continue for **Head:** Beg with a P row, work even in St st for 11 rows. *Next row:* K2 tog across to last st, end K1—14 sts. P and bind off. **Arms:** Using dark brown and starting at upper end, cast on 8 sts. Work even in St st for 4 rows. Cut dark brown, tie on light brown and use to K 1 row, P 1 row. **Complete as Follows:** Cut yarn, leaving a long end. Thread into yarn needle and pull through sts as they are taken off knitting needle. **Legs:** Using dark brown and starting at upper end, cast on 8 sts. Work even in St st for 8 rows. Cut dark brown, tie on light brown, and K 1 row. P 1 row. Complete as for arms. **Ears:**

(make four pieces—two for each ear): Starting at lower edge, with light brown, cast on 4 sts. Work even in St st for 3 rows. *Next row:* P2 tog twice. Cut yarn, leaving long end. Thread into yarn needle and pull through rem 2 sts as they are taken off knitting needle. Sew these 2 sts firmly down to top of ear piece, at the same time rounding the top of ear. Run in end on wrong side to hide, and clip off. **Nose:** Using light brown yarn, cast on 12 sts. Work St st for 2 rows. Complete

as for arms and legs, pulling yarn through sts as they are taken from knitting needle.

Finishing:

Finish, sew together and embroider the face in same manner as for Father Bear and Mother Bear.

To make pants:

Using pattern, cut two pants pieces from red felt. Sew the two pieces

together for front, from top down to crotch. Repeat for back seam. Fold flat with seams at front and back. Sew leg seam, matching the other seams at crotch. Turn right side out. Put on bear. Turn up cuffs. For straps, measure and cut two pieces from bias binding to fit over shoulders (plus a little to tuck under pants top). Sew in place, ends under top of pants. Sew a small button just below where each strap joins pants on front. Omit buttons for a very young child.

Patterns for Bears

Pants (for Father Bear)

Pants (for Baby Bear)

(place left edge of each pattern on fold)

Four Big Dolls

I'd like to introduce four dolls: Sally, a doll dressed in a red skirt with an apron, who wears a kerchief over long black hair; Betsy, a doll with brown hair dressed in a blue skirt with a flowered apron; Maggie, a doll in a green skirt with an eyelet apron and a mob cap over short curly brown hair, and Bonnie, a doll with long blonde hair and a braid around her head, dressed in a long flowered skirt.

Each doll is about 15 inches tall and very huggable.

To make Sally you'll need:

Acrylic yarn of knitting worsted weight:
- ½ oz white
- 1 oz red
- 1 oz light pink
- 1 oz black
- Small amount of brown (for shoes)

Fabric:
- ¼ yd of red and white polka-dot fabric (for skirt and kerchief)
- 5¼ × 8 in piece of red and white striped (for apron—I used pillow ticking)

9 in of wide white bias tape (for waistband)

Felt: very small piece of brown (for eyes)

Embroidery floss: small amount of red and brown

1 pair #4 knitting needles

Stitch holder

Yarn needle

Sewing thread to match fabric, felt, and hair

Sewing needle

Polyester fiberfill

12 in long piece of cardboard

To make Betsy you'll need:

Acrylic yarn of knitting worsted weight:
- 1 oz white
- 1 oz blue
- 1 oz light pink
- ½ oz brown
- Small amount of black (for shoes)

Fabric:
- 6 × 20 in. piece of blue (for skirt)
- 5 × 10 in piece of small blue flowered print
- 3 × 4 in piece of the same print

21 in of ½-inch orange bias tape

14 in narrow white ribbon

Felt: very small piece of brown for eyes

Embroidery floss: small amounts of red and brown

2 small orange buttons

1 pair #4 knitting needles

Stitch holder

Yarn needle

Sewing thread to match fabric, felt, and hair

Sewing needle

Polyester fiberfill

12 in long piece of cardboard

To make Maggie you'll need:

Acrylic yarn of knitting worsted weight:
- ½ oz white
- 1 oz light green
- 1 oz light pink
- ½ oz brown
- Small amount of black (for shoes)

Fabric:
- ¼ yd green print (for skirt and cap)
- 4¼ × 11 in piece of white eyelet (for apron)
- 8 in square piece of pink (for cap lining)

21 in of 1-inch pink flowered braid

12 in narrow pink ribbon (for cap)

12 in narrow elastic

Felt: very small piece of brown for eyes

Embroidery floss: small amount of red and brown

1 pair #4 knitting needles

Stitch holder

Yarn needle

Sewing thread to match fabric, felt, and hair

Sewing needle
Polyester fiberfill
6½ in long piece of cardboard

To make Bonnie you'll need:

Acrylic yarn of knitting worsted
    weight:
    1½ oz white
    1 oz light pink
    ½ oz yellow
    Small amount of red (for shoes)
Fabric: 8 × 20 in piece of blue
    flowered material (for skirt)
9 in of 1-inch wide red ribbon
Felt:
    Small piece of brown (for eyes)
    Piece of blue (for vest) about
        9 in square
2 small white motifs (cut from
    "by the yard" braid) or 2
    small buttons (for front of
    vest)
A few small artificial flowers for
    hair

Embroidery floss: small amounts
    of red and brown
1 pair #4 knitting needles
Stitch holder
Yarn needle
Sewing thread to match fabric, felt,
    and hair
Sewing needle
Polyester fiberfill
12 in-long piece of cardboard

All four dolls are made in the
same general manner, with the
panties, blouse, shoes and stockings knit-on. Two pieces are knitted alike for the front and back
of the body and head. The arms
and legs are each knit in one piece.
All are sewn up, stuffed, turned
right side out, assembled and
dressed.

Make Sally:

Body (make two alike—front and
back): Starting at lower edge of
panties with white, cast on 20 sts.
Work in garter st for 6 rows.
Change to St st. Beg with P row,
work even for 11 rows (the knit
side is the right side). *Next row*
Waistline: P 1 row on right side.
Next row (dec row): P2 tog across
row—10 sts. *Next row:* P 1 row
on right side. Cut white, tie on
red for blouse and P 1 row. *Next
row:* K and inc 1 st in each st
across—20 sts. Beg with P row,
work even in St st for 17 rows.
Shape Shoulders: Bind off 5 sts
at beg of next 2 rows—10 sts.
Change to garter st and work 5
rows. Cut red and tie on pink.
Next row **Head:** P4, inc 1 st in
next st, P5—11 sts. *Next row:* K
and inc 1 st in each st across row—
22 sts. Beg with P row, work
even in St st for 22 rows (ending
with a knit row). P 1 row, dec
1 st each end—20 sts. Dec for
top of head: *Row 1:* K2 tog
across—10 sts; *Row 2:* P2 tog
across—5 sts; *Row 3:* K2 tog, K1,

Racquel Raccoon with Betty and Billy Bunny.

The Christmas Mouse with Santa Bear of Sixteen Little Bears.

The House Mouse of Two Nice Mice with Puss in Boots.

Four Puppy Dogs' Spot with the Country Kids.

Betsy of Four Big Dolls (*center*) with (*left to right*) Mistress Mary, Alice in Wonderland, Little Red Riding Hood, and Little Boy Blue of Eight Little Dolls.

Goldilocks and the Three Bears with Polar Bear and Sweetheart Bear of Sixteen Little Bears.

ABOVE:
Sailor Boy and Girl with Rose Red and Rose White of Eight Little Dolls.

Baby Bunting, with Koala Bear and Brown Bear of Sixteen Little Bears sitting in her basket.

Girl and Boy Bedtime Bears (*center*), flanked by Brother (*left*) and
Sister (*right*) Black Bears, all of Sixteen Little Bears.

Brown Bear and Beige Bear of Three Bears posing with (*left to right*)
Brown Bear with Scarf, Brown Bear with Bikini, Golden Bear with
Flower Chain, and Golden Bear in Green Vest of Sixteen Little Bears.

Patches, Ginger, and Blackie of Four Puppy Dogs posing
with Three Little Kittens and Mother Cat.

Bonnie of Four Big Dolls.

Two Clowns and a friend, Clown Bear of Sixteen Small Bears.

**Sally and Maggie
of Four Big Dolls
with Hansel and Gretel
of Eight Little Dolls.**

Benjamin Bear with the Roly-Poly Family.

A panda bear trio: Panda Bear of Three Bears (*center*) with
Panda with Red Bandana and Panda with Sailor Collar
of Sixteen Little Bears.

K2 tog—3 sts. Cut yarn, leaving a long end for sewing. **To Complete:** Thread yarn into yarn needle and pull through sts as you take them off knitting needles. **Arms** (make two): Beg at top of blouse sleeve, with red, cast on 14 sts. Work in garter st for 2 rows. *Next row:* K and inc 1 st in each st across—28 sts. Work garter st 12 rows more. *Next row* (first dec row): K2 tog across—14 sts. Cut red, tie on pink for arm and beg with P row, work St st for 3 rows. *Next row* (second dec row): K3, K2 tog, K4, K2 tog, K3—12 sts. Beg with P row, work 15 rows even in St st. *Next row* **Shape Hand:** *K2 tog, K1, repeat from * across row—8 sts. P 1 row. *Next row* (inc row): *inc 1 st in next st, K1, repeat from * across row—12 sts. Beg with P row, work 6 rows even in St st. *Next row:* P2 tog across row—6 sts. K and bind off. **Legs** (make two): Starting at top with black for stockings, cast on 16 sts. Work 12 rows in St st. *Next row* (first dec row): K4, K2 tog, K4, K2 tog, K4—14 sts. Beg with P row, work St st for 11 rows more. *Next row* (second dec row): K3, K2 tog, K4, K2 tog, K3—12 sts. Beg with P row, work 7 rows more in St st. *Next row* (third dec row): K3, K2 tog, K2, K2 tog, K3—10 sts. P 1 row. Cut black, tie on brown. *Next row* **Shoe:** K across row. *Next row:* P across 5 sts, put rem 5 sts onto st holder to be worked later for second half of shoe. *Next row:* working on first side only, cast on 4 sts at beg of row, K across—9 sts. Beg with P row, work 5 rows in St st. K and bind off. **Second Half of Shoe:** Put sts from holder onto left-hand needle, with point at middle of leg. Tie on brown and P across row. K 1 row. *Next row:* Cast on 4 sts at beg of row, P across row—9 sts. Work even in St st for 4 rows. K and bind off.

Finishing:

Body and Head: With right sides together, use matching yarn and back stitch to sew the two pieces together, close along edges, leaving bottom edge open. Turn right side out and stuff firmly, shaping as you stuff. Overcast opening closed. **Arms:** Fold arm piece in half, wrong side out, and sew seam as for body and head, leaving top open. Turn to right side by pushing the hand inside and continuing to push until it comes out of the top. Stuff firmly and sew closed by gathering top edge together. Sew in place with seam at underside of arm. At underarm, take a few stitches from sleeve to body of blouse to hold arm down close to body. **Legs:** Fold and sew as for arms, sewing shoe sides together down around front, across bottom and up back. Sew remainder back seam, leaving top open. Turn by pushing shoe through to top. Stuff firmly and sew closed straight across top, toes to front. Sew in place at bottom of body. **Hair:** Wind black yarn around a 12 in cardboard 40 times. Slip carefully off cardboard, and lay all loops flat. Cut a piece of yarn 12 in long, and use to tie all strands together at center into a loose, flat bundle that measures about 2½″ across. Carefully pick up bundle and place on head with tying yarn at center top of head for "part" in the hair. Secure in place by sewing down to head with back stitch along the part. Arrange hair around sides and back of head and sew down to head a little above neckline. Do not cut loops: leave them for curls. **Face:** Using pattern, cut eyes from brown felt. Sew in place, with matching thread, using back stitch. Using a double strand of brown floss and outline stitch, embroider heavy eyebrows right above eyes. Use a single strand of red floss and outline stitch to make mouth and a very small nose.

Make clothes:

Skirt: From red and white polka-dot fabric, cut a 6 by 20 in piece. With right side inside, sew the two short ends together. Make a ½ in hem on one long side. Turn down the other long side on inside about ¼ in and gather to fit doll's waist. Turn right side out and put on doll with seam at center back. Sew gathered edge to doll at waistline. **Apron:** Make a small hem on three sides of the 5¼ in by 8 in red and white striped fabric. On the fourth side, make a ½ in hem for bottom of apron. Gather top side to be about 3½ in across and sew in place over skirt at waistline. Wrap the wide white bias tape around waistline over top of skirt and apron. Sew ends together in back, folding raw edges inside. **Kerchief:** Using pattern, cut kerchief from red and white polka-dot fabric. Make a narrow hem on all edges. Place on doll's head and sew ends in place under chin by sewing through to doll.

Make Betsy:

Body (make two): Follow directions for Sally, using white for panties and using blue instead of red for blouse. Work even in St st for 18 rows instead of 17 (ending with knit row). **Shape Shoulders:** Bind off 5 sts at beg of next 2 rows—10 sts. *Next row:* K 1 row on wrong side. Cut blue, tie on pink for **Head:** K1 row. P 1 row. *Next row:* K4, inc 1 st in next st, K5—11 sts. P 1 row. *Next row:* K and inc 1 st in each st across—22 sts. Beg with P row, work even in St st for 22 rows. *Next row:* P and dec 1 st at each end—20 sts. Dec for top of head and complete as for Sally. **Arms:** Beg at top with blue, cast on 14 sts. K 1 row. P 1 row. *Next row:* K and inc 1 st in each st across—28 sts. Beg with P row, work even in St st for 13 rows. *Next row:* K2 tog across—14 sts. *Next row:* K 1 row on wrong side. Cut blue, tie on pink and work 4 rows even in St st. *Next row* (second dec row): K3, K2 tog, K4, K2 tog, K3—12 sts. Beg with P row work for 15 rows. **Shape Hand:** Same as for Sally. **Legs:** Follow directions for Sally, using white (instead of black) for stockings and black (instead of brown) for shoes.

Finishing:

Body and Head: Follow the directions for Sally to sew together, stuff, and assemble the body and head pieces, arms and legs. Make and sew on the hair and face in the same way, using brown yarn for the hair instead of black.

Make clothes:

Skirt: With the wrong side out, sew the two short ends of skirt piece together. Sew a ½ in hem on one long side. Turn the other side, about ¼ in to inside and gather up to fit the doll's waistline. Turn right side out, put on the doll with seam at center back and sew the gathered edge to doll at waistline. **Apron:** On two short sides and one long side of the 5 in by 10 in print fabric make ¼ in hems. Make a ½ in hem on other long side for bottom edge. Fold 3 in × 4 in piece in half wrong side out to be 3 in × 2 in. Make a narrow seam along each 2 in side. Turn to right side and slip stitch bottom edge closed. Gather top of larger piece to measure about 5½ in across. Center smaller piece on this edge for bib of apron. Sew these two apron pieces together and sew in place on doll over skirt. Measure and cut two pieces of orange bias tape for straps to fit from top of bib, over shoulders, cross in back, down to top of skirt. Sew in place. Measure and cut a piece of orange bias to fit around doll's waist over skirt and apron. Sew in place, folding ends over in back and covering ends of straps. Sew a button in place at each top corner of bib over where straps are attached. Make white ribbon into bow and sew to top of head.

Make Maggie:

Body (make two alike): Follow directions exactly as for Sally, for body and head, using light green for blouse instead of red. **Arms:** Make as for Sally, using green instead of red for sleeves. **Legs:** Starting at top with green, cast on 16 sts. Work 2 rows in St st. Drop green, but do not cut. Tie on white for stripes and use to work 2 rows in St st. Repeat these 4 rows twice for a total of 12 rows, alternating colors every 2 rows and carrying yarn not in use up side of work. *Next row:* (first dec row): With green, K4, K2 tog, K4, K2 tog, K4—14 sts. P 1 row with green. Work 10 rows more in St st, alternating colors as before. *Next row:* (second dec row): With green, K3, K2 tog, K4, K2 tog, K3—12 sts. P 1 row with green. Work 6 rows more in St st, alternating colors. *Next row:* (third dec row): With green, K3, K2 tog, K2, K2 tog, K3—10 sts. P 1 row with green. Cut both green and white, tie on black and make shoe as for Sally.

Finishing:

Body: Follow the directions for Sally to sew together, stuff and assemble the body and head pieces, arms and legs. **Note:** Be extra careful to match stripes at back of legs. Make the face same as for Sally, also. **To Make Hair:** Wind brown yarn around a 6½ in cardboard 40 times. Slip all loops carefully off cardboard and lay flat. Do not cut loops: leave them for curls. With a 10 in strand of yarn, tie around all strands at center into a loose, flat bundle measuring about 2½ in across, for "part" in the hair. Place on head and sew down using back stitch along the part, at center top of head. Arrange hair around sides and back of head and sew in place around head a little above all curl ends. Using extra yarn in yarn needle, you can make and fill in extra loops for more curls around face and hairline, if you wish.

Make clothes:

Skirt: Cut a 6½ × 22 in rectangle from green print fabric. Make and sew onto doll same as for Sally. Make apron in same manner, omitting hem if eyelet already has a finished bottom edge. Gather top to 4 in across and sew in place over skirt at waistline. Measure and cut a piece of flowered braid trim to fit around waistline, and two pieces for shoulder straps. Sew all in place, tucking ends of straps under waistband. **Mob Cap:** Using pattern, cut one piece for cap from same fabric as skirt and one piece for lining from pink fabric. Holding right sides together, sew together with a ¼ in seam, leaving a small space for turning. Turn to right side and slip stitch opening closed. 1 in in from outer edge make a line of stitching for casing all around cap. Make a second line in same manner ¼ in outside of first line leaving a small space unstitched. Run narrow elastic through casing, pull up to fit doll's head. Tie ends and sew opening closed. Make a bow with pink ribbon and sew to back of cap over casing lines. Put cap on head.

Make Bonnie:

Body (two pieces alike): Using white, follow directions for Sally to make panties through waistline dec row, until there are 10 sts left on needle. P 2 rows even. *Next row:* K and inc 1 st in each st across—20 sts. Continuing with white for blouse, start pattern st: *Row 1* (wrong side): K across. *Row 2:* K1, P1 across. Repeat these 2 rows for a total of 18 rows of pattern st, ending with Row 2 (a front-side row). **Shape Shoulders:** Continuing in pattern, bind off 5 sts at beg of next 2 rows—10 sts. K 1 row on wrong side. Cut white, tie on pink for **Head**. K 1 row, P 1 row. *Next row:* K4, inc 1 st in next st, K5—11 sts. *Next row:* P across. *Next row:* K and inc 1 st in each st across—22 sts. Beg with P row, work even in St st for 22 rows, then dec and finish as for Sally. **Arms:** Beg at top of sleeve, with white, cast on 14 sts. Work 2 rows of pattern st as for blouse. *Next*

row: K and inc 1 st in each st across—28 sts. Starting with Row 2 of pattern, work pattern for 13 rows more. *Next row:* K2 tog across—14 sts. Cut white, tie on pink and work arm and hand as for Sally. **Legs:** Follow directions for Sally, using white instead of black for stockings and red instead of brown for shoes.

Finishing:

Follow the directions for Sally to sew together, stuff, and assemble the body and head pieces, arms, and legs. Make the face in the same way, also. **Hair:** Using yellow yarn, make hair and sew to head as for Sally. Next, make a braid to circle head on top of hair just sewn on: cut 21 strands of yarn, each 18 in long. Separate strands into three groups of seven each, and braid

together. Measure braid to fit around head and trim if necessary, tying a strand of yarn tightly around each end of braid to hold. Place around head, with ends meeting at center back, and sew in place with matching thread. Sew a few small artificial flowers very securely at one side of head over braid and a few at center back of head.

Make clothes:

Skirt: Using blue flowered material, make and sew skirt to doll as for Sally. Sew red ribbon around waistline, over top of skirt, ends overlapping at center back. **Vest:** Using pattern, cut vest from blue felt. Sew side and shoulder seams. Turn right side out and put on doll. Sew the two small white mo-

tifs onto front edges of vest, side by side, sewing them together to hold vest closed. Buttons may be used instead.

Patterns for Four Big Dolls

Eye (for all four dolls)

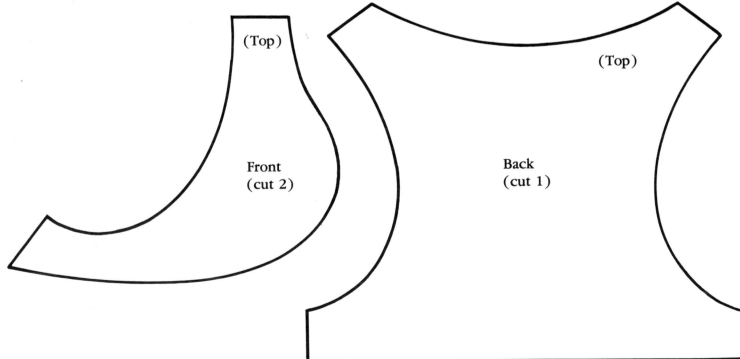

Vest (for Bonnie)

(Top)

Front
(cut 2)

(Top)

Back
(cut 1)

Kerchief (for Sally)

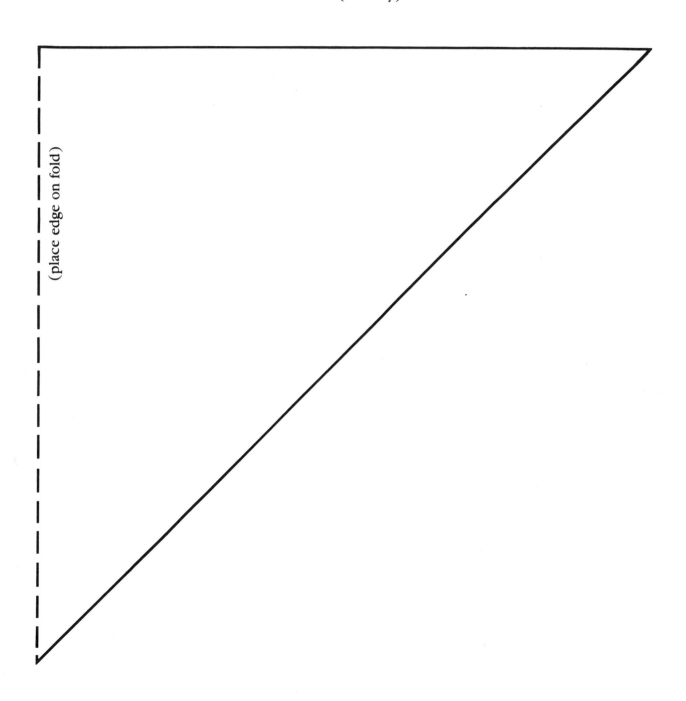

(place edge on fold)

Mob cap (for Maggie)

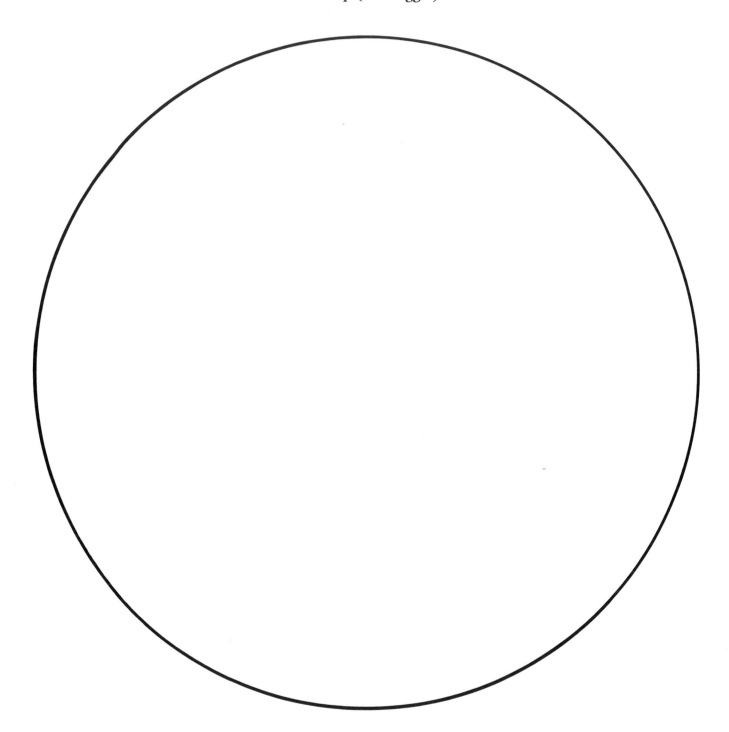

Four Puppy Dogs

These cute dogs all have familiar names that tell us how they look. They are Ginger, Spot, Blackie, and Patches. Each one is 11 inches tall, and all are made in the same general way. The only exceptions are the length of ears and the tails, and Patches wears a knit-on sweater with colorful sewn-on patches of fabric.

To make Ginger you'll need:

Acrylic yarn of knitting worsted weight: 3 oz gold
1 yd of 1-inch wide colorful braid
Small pieces of brown and white felt
Embroidery floss: very small amount of brown
1 pair #4 knitting needles
Yarn needle
Sewing thread to match or contrast with felt and braid
Sewing needle
Polyester fiberfill

To make Spot you'll need:

Acrylic yarn of knitting worsted weight:
  2½ oz off-white
  ½ oz brown
21 in of red plaid ribbon, ¾-in wide
Felt: small pieces of medium blue, dark blue, black, and brown
Embroidery floss: very small amount of black
1 pair #4 knitting needles
Yarn needle
Sewing thread to match or contrast with felt
Sewing needle
Polyester fiberfill

To make Blackie you'll need:

Acrylic yarn of knitting worsted weight:
  2½ oz black
  ½ oz white
12 in of ¾-inch red braid
Felt: small pieces of brown, white, and gray
1 small "brass" buckle
Embroidery floss: very small amount of brown
1 pair #4 knitting needles
Yarn needle
Sewing thread to match or contrast with felt and braid
Sewing needle
Polyester fiberfill

To make Patches you'll need:

Acrylic yarn of knitting worsted weight:
  2 oz gray
  1 oz dark red
Fabric: several scrap pieces in different colors and patterns
Felt: small pieces of brown and white
Embroidery floss: very small amount of brown

1 pair #4 knitting needles
Yarn needle
Sewing thread to match felt and fabric
Sewing needle
Polyester fiberfill

The body and head piece, the arms, legs, ears, and tail are each made and then sewn together. Finally, the features are added, and each puppy is then dressed up a bit with added trim.

Make Ginger:

Body and Head (one piece): Starting at lower edge of body, cast on 40 sts. Work even in St st for 32 rows. (The knit side is the right side.) *Next row* (inc row): *K1, inc 1 st in next st, repeat from * across row—60 sts. Continue for **Head:** Beg with P row, work even in St st for 26 rows. *Next row:* P2 tog across—30 sts. *Next row:* K and bind off. **Arms** (make two): Starting at upper end, cast on 20 sts. Work even in St st for 14 rows (knit side is right side). *Next row:* K2 tog across row—10 sts. P 1 row. **Complete as fol-**

lows: Cut yarn, leaving long end for sewing. Thread yarn into yarn needle and pull through sts as you take them off knitting needle. **Legs** (make two): Starting at upper end, cast on 20 sts. Work even in St st for 22 rows (the knit side is right side). *Next row:* K2 tog across row—10 sts. P 1 row. Complete as for arms. **Ears** (make four pieces—two for each ear): Starting at top of ear, cast on 8 sts. K 1 row. P 1 row (the knit side is the right side). *Next row:* K and inc 1 st at beg and end of row. P 1 row. Repeat last two rows twice—14 sts. Work even in St st for 10 rows. *Next row* (dec row): Work across and dec 1 st at beg and end of row. Continuing in St st, repeat dec row on every row, 4 times, until 4 sts remain on needle. P and bind off. **Tail** (make one): (Tail is made crosswise, and the purl side is the right side.) Cast on 12 sts. Work even in St st for 8 rows. K and bind off.

Finishing:

Body and Head: Bring sides of piece together (right side out) to form a tube. Using matching yarn and overcast stitch, seam sides together. Fold piece flat, with seam down center back. Sew closed across top of head. Stuff firmly. Sew closed across bottom edge. **To Form Neckline:** Thread a long length of matching yarn into yarn needle. Working on inc row, take a few stitches to secure yarn at back seam. Wrap yarn around dog twice, pulling hard to pull piece in to form neck. Hold firmly and return to where yarn was secured, and secure again with several stitches. Clip yarn and hide end in work. **Arms:** Thread yarn that was pulled through last stitches of arm into yarn needle. Pull up tightly, bringing sides together right side out and forming a tube. Fasten securely. Take a few stitches to close this outer end completely. Sew seam, where

sides were brought together with overcast stitch. Stuff firmly. To finish upper end, run yarn in and out around cast on edge to gather. Pull up to close and fasten. Sew onto dog at side of body with seam at underside. **Legs:** Finish lower end of legs as for outer end of arms. Sew seam and stuff firmly. Fold upper end flat and sew straight across to close, with seam at center back or inside of leg. Sew in place at lower edge of dog's body. **Ears:** Hold two pieces for each ear together with right sides out. Using matching yarn, overcast them together around all edges to make one ear. Place on sides of head with cast-on edge across end of head seam. Sew to head across top of ear and down back and front edges for about an inch to secure. The rest of the ear hangs free. **Tail:** Allow piece to roll up (as it naturally will), with purl side out. Thread matching yarn into needle and run in and out on one short side of piece to gather for end of tail. Pull tight, fasten and sew closed. Sew seam along length of tail by sewing bound-off edge to cast-on edge. This will pull tail up into a natural curl. Stuff. Sew end closed and sew in place at back of dog. **Face:** Using patterns, cut two large eye pieces from white felt and two smaller eye pieces from brown felt. Cut one nose piece from brown felt. Sew in place, with smaller eye piece on top of larger piece, the larger piece extending above the smaller one. Sew nose in place. Use either matching or contrasting thread, and back stitch. Using embroidery floss and outline stitch, make mouth, extending down and curving out below nose.

Harness:

Cut a piece of braid trim long enough to go around middle of body plus ½ in to fold under. Cut two pieces to go over shoulders, long enough to reach from front to back of body piece, plus ½ in at each end to tuck under. Cut a short piece to go across chest between shoulder pieces at upper front. Cut a second short piece to go across upper back between shoulder pieces. Sew all in place and together, using matching thread and taking a few stitches through to body of dog to hold in place.

Make Spot:

Body: Using the off-white yarn follow directions for making body and head piece, arms and legs the same as for Ginger. **Ears:** These

are longer and are made in two pieces, one for each ear. Using brown yarn, starting at top edge of ear, cast on 6 sts. K 1 row. *Next row:* K and inc 1 st in each st across—12 sts. Work even in garter st for 40 rows. K and bind off. **Tail:** This tail is a longer one, made crosswise. (The purl side is the right side.) Using brown, cast on 24 sts. Work even in St st for 8 rows. K and bind off.

Finishing:

Body and Head: Finish, stuff and sew together body and head piece, arms, legs, and tail the same as for Ginger. **Ears:** At bound-off edge of ear, fold up each side of end to meet on back side of ear, thus forming a point at end of ear. Sew together to back of ear. Place cast-on edge across end of head seam. Sew to head by sewing across top and down back and front edges for about an inch to secure. Allow the rest of the ear to hang free. **Face:** Make face in same manner as for Ginger, making larger eye pieces from medium blue, small eye pieces from dark blue and nose from black felt. Embroider mouth with black floss. Using patterns, cut three different sizes of spots from brown felt—as many as you like of each. Place on body wherever you please and sew in place, using matching thread and back stitch. Tie ribbon around neck with bow at front.

Make Blackie:

Body: Using black yarn, follow directions for making body and

head piece, arms and legs the same as for Ginger. Using white yarn, follow directions for making the longer ears and tail like Spot's.

Finishing:

Body and Head: Follow directions to finish, stuff, and sew together the body and head piece, arms, legs, and tail, just as for Ginger. Follow directions to finish ears as for Spot. **Face:** Make face as for Ginger, making larger eye pieces from white and small eye pieces from brown felt. Make nose from gray felt, and embroider mouth with brown floss. Sew "brass" buckle to one end of red braid. Place braid around neck and pull the other end through buckle, pulling up tight to fit.

Make Patches:

Body and Head (one piece): Starting at lower edge of body with gray, cast on 40 sts. Work even in St st for 8 rows. Cut gray. Tie on dark red for sweater and work in garter st for 6 rows. Change to St st and work 16 rows even. Change back to garter st and work 4 rows. Cut red, tie on gray for **Head** and beg with inc row, work it and continue on to **Head** and finish as for Ginger. **Arms** (make two): Starting at top, with dark red for sleeve, cast on 20 sts. Work in St st for 4 rows. Change to garter st and work 4 rows. Cut red, tie on gray for arm and work 6 rows in St st. *Next row:* K2 tog across—10 sts. P 1 row. Complete as for Ginger. Make legs, ears and tail according to directions for Ginger, using gray yarn for all.

Finishing:

Body and Head: Follow directions as for Ginger to sew, stuff and assemble, body and head piece, arms, legs, ears and tail.
Face: Follow the same directions as for Ginger, using same colors.
Decorate Sweater: Cut out many patches from fabric in various sizes and colors; as many as you wish. Sew each onto sweater part of dog—wherever you like—to make a colorful pup.

Patterns for Four Puppy Dogs

Outer eye (for all four dogs)
and
Large spot (for Spot)

Inner eye (for all four dogs)
and
Medium spot (for Spot)

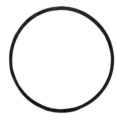

Small spot (for Spot)

Nose (for all four dogs)

Gingerbread Boy and Girl

Here is a Gingerbread pair: a boy and a girl who match. Each one is brown with the usual white "gingerbread" trim. They are dressed in denim with colorful shoulder straps. He has a red bowtie, and she wears a red ribbon at the top of her head. They are 13 inches tall. Once trimmed and dressed, they make a soft toy to play with and a good companion to take to bed.

To make the Gingerbread Boy you'll need:

Acrylic yarn of knitting worsted weight: 3 oz medium brown
⅛ yd blue denim
15 in of 1-inch wide striped ribbon (for straps)
48 in of medium width white rick rack
2 in of narrow width red rick rack
White felt circles or flower trim (something that can be cut apart for eyes and nose): about 6 in
6 in of medium width red grosgrain ribbon (for bowtie)
1 pair #4 knitting needles
Yarn needle
Stitch holder
Sewing thread to match fabric, trims, and ribbons
Sewing needle
Polyester fiberfill

To make the Gingerbread Girl you'll need:

The same materials as for the boy with the few following exceptions:

1) About 15 in of inch-wide colorful braid (for straps) instead of striped ribbon.
2) An additional 10 in of fancy white braid (for neckband).
3) 12 in of red grosgrain ribbon (for hair bow) instead of 6 in.
4) If cut from a 44-45 inch bolt, the ⅛ yd of denim required for the boy's pants will also be enough to make the girl's skirt.

Both are made in the same way by knitting two pieces alike for the front and back of the entire body. These two pieces are sewn together.

Make the Gingerbread Boy:

Body (make two): Starting at top of head, cast on 10 sts. P 1 row. *Next row:* (right side): K and inc 1 st in each st across row—20 sts. P 1 row.   Continue to work in St st and inc 1 st each end of each knit row until there are 30 sts on needle.   Beg with P row, work even in St st for 5 rows.   K and inc 1 st each end of next row—32 sts.   Beg with P row, work even for 7 rows. *Next row:* K and dec 1 st each end. P 1 row. Repeat last 2 rows once—28 sts. *Next row:* K and dec 1 st each end—26 sts.   Continue in St st and dec 1 st each end of next 5 rows—16 sts. **Arms:** Continue in St st and cast on 16 sts at beg of next 2 rows—48 sts. *Next row:* K and inc 1 st each end. Continue in St st and inc 1 st each end of each row until there are 56 sts on needle, ending with a P row. Work 8 rows even. *Next row* (dec row): work and dec 1 st each end of row.   Continue to work in St st and continue to dec 1 st each end of each row until 48 sts remain on needle.   At beg of next 2 rows, bind off 12 sts—24 sts. Work even for 4 rows. *Next row:* K and inc 1 st each end of row. P 1 row.   Repeat last 2 rows, twice—30 sts. Work even on body for 10 rows. *Next row:* **Divide for Legs:** inc 1 st in first st, K across 14 more sts.   Put rem 15 sts onto st holder for second leg. **First Leg:** Beg with P row, work even in St st on 16 sts for 21 rows. *Next row:* (dec for toe): K and dec 1 st each end of row. *Next*

row: P and dec 1 st each end of row.   Repeat last 2 rows until 4 sts remain on needle. K and bind off.   **Second Leg:** Put sts from holder onto needle with point at center of body. Tie on yarn, K across 15 sts, inc 1 st in last st—16 sts. Work as for first leg.

Finishing:

Body and Head: Holding right sides together, using matching yarn and back stitch, sew the two body pieces together, close along outside edges, leaving opening between legs for stuffing. Turn right side out, stuff firmly, and overcast opening closed. Place white rick-rack continuously around all edges of front side. Sew in place. Sew a short strip of white circle braid down center front from neckline to just below waistline. Cut circles off from additional trim, and sew two in place for eyes and one for nose. (These can be cut from felt if you wish.) Sew the narrow red rick-rack on for mouth, curving it into a smile.

Make clothes:

Pants: Using pattern for pants, cut the four pieces from denim. Making ¼ in seams, sew two pieces for front together from top edge down to crotch. Sew remaining two pieces together in same manner for back. Sew inside leg seams. Next, hem top of back and front and both legs at bottom edge before sewing side seams: it is much

easier this way. **Hems:** turn under ⅜ in once and sew down in place. Now, as the last step, sew ¼ in seams at the sides. Pull pants onto Gingerbread Boy—they should fit tightly. Measure and cut ribbon for straps and sew in place, tucking ends under top of pants. Make a bow tie of red grosgrain ribbon and sew in place on front at neckline.

Make the Gingerbread Girl:

Body: K and finish the body exactly as for the boy, sewing on the white rick-rack, the braid down the front, the eyes, nose, and mouth in the same manner. Place the 10 in of white braid around neck and take a few stitches to hold in place. Make a bow of the red ribbon and sew in place at top of head.

Make skirt:

Using pattern for skirt, cut the four pieces from denim. Making ¼ in seams, sew two pieces together for center front. Sew remaining two pieces together in same manner for back. Next, hem top and bottom edges of both front and back pieces by turning under ⅜ in once and sew in place. Sew ¼ in side seams. Pull skirt up over legs, in place onto Gingerbread Girl. Using the colorful braid trim for straps, measure, cut, and sew in place as for the boy.

Patterns for Gingerbread Boy and Girl

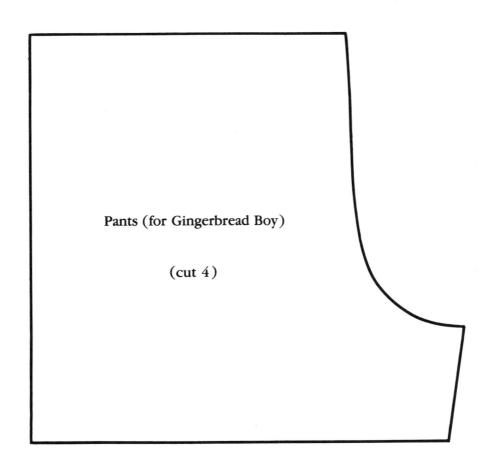

Pants (for Gingerbread Boy)

(cut 4)

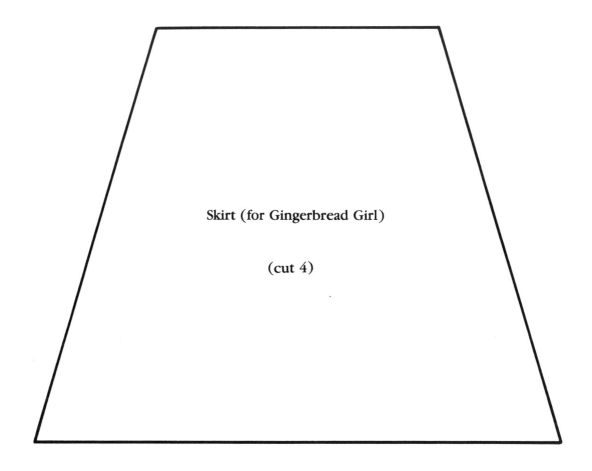

Skirt (for Gingerbread Girl)

(cut 4)

Two Clowns

Here is a big clown about 17 inches tall and a smaller one about 14 inches tall (not counting his hat—that adds another 2 inches). They are both, like most clowns everywhere, very colorful, with big smiling faces, orange hair, and multi-colored clothes.

To make the larger clown you'll need:

Acrylic yarn of knitting worsted weight
    ¾ oz red
    ¾ oz light blue
    ¾ oz off-white
    ¾ oz dark blue
    ¾ oz green
    ¾ oz variegated red
    ¼ oz orange (for hair)
    If you should run out of a color, just substitute any other color you like—it will only make a more colorful clown.
25 in of ¾-in-wide red-and-white polkadot ribbon
Felt: small pieces of red, pink, and navy blue
1 pair #6 knitting needles
Yarn needle
Sewing thread to match ribbon, felt, and hair
Sewing needle
Polyester fiberfill
9-in-long piece of cardboard

To make the smaller clown you'll need:

Acrylic yarn of knitting worsted weight:

2½ oz off-white
2 oz variegated
¾ oz medium blue
¼ oz orange (for hair)
1 yd of 1-inch-wide red and white ruffled trim
Felt:
    2 pieces of orange 3 × 5 in (for front and back)

1 piece of orange 3½ × 5 in (for sleeve)
2 pieces of yellow 3 × 5 in (for front and back)
1 piece of yellow 3½ × 5 in (for sleeve)
Very small pieces of red and medium blue (for eyes, nose, and mouth)

Note: All orange and yellow pieces can each be cut from one 9 × 12 in piece of felt.
7 red pom-poms
1 pair #4 and 1 pair #6 knitting needles
Stitch holder
Yarn needle
Sewing thread to match felt, trim, and pom-poms
Sewing needle
Polyester fiberfill

The body and head of each is made in two pieces exactly alike. The arms of both are each made of one piece. The legs of the larger clown are each made of two pieces, sewn together at front and back. The legs of the smaller clown are each made of one piece only, sewn together up the back. The facial features of each are made entirely of felt, and the hair is yarn. They are dressed mostly in knit clothes—either knit-on or knitted separately, but the smaller clown wears a shirt made of felt, and each has different trims added for additional appeal.

Make the larger clown:

Body and Head (make two): Beg at lower edge of body, with red for underpants, cast on 20 sts. Work even in St st for 18 rows. (The knit side is the right side.) Cut red, tie on light blue for shirt and change to garter st and work even for 22 rows. Cut blue, tie on off-white for neck and head. *Next row:* K2 tog across row—10 sts. P 1 row, K 1 row, P 1 row. Continue on in St st. *Next row* **Head:** K and inc 1 st each end of this row and each K row until

there are 20 sts on needle. Beg with P row, work even in St st for 9 rows. *Next row:* K and dec 1 st each end of row. P 1 row. Repeat last two rows 3 times—12 sts. *Next row:* K2 tog across row—6 sts. Purl and bind off. **Arms** (make two): Beg at upper end of sleeve, with light blue, cast on 14 sts. Work even in garter st for 26 rows. Cut blue, tie on off-white for hand. *Next row:* K2 tog across row—7 sts. P 1 row. *Next row:* K and inc 1 st in each st across—14 sts. Beg with P row, work even in St st for 5 rows (the knit side is the right side). *Next row:* K2 tog, K3, K2 tog (twice), K3, K2 tog—10 sts. *Next row:* P2 tog across—5 sts. K and bind off. **Legs—First side** (make two—one for each leg): Beg at bottom of shoe with red, cast on 14 sts. Work in garter st for 8 rows. *Next row:* K2 tog (twice), K10—12 sts. *Next row:* K4, K2 tog (4 times)—8 sts. K 1 row even. Cut red, tie on variegated red for stocking leg and work in St st for 40 rows (the knit side is the right side). K and bind off. **Second Side of Leg** (make two—one for each leg): With red for shoe, cast on 14 sts. Work in garter st for 8 rows. *Next row:* K10, K2 tog (twice)—12 sts. *Next row:* K2 tog (4 times), K4—8 sts. K 1 row. Cut red, tie on variegated red for stocking leg and work even in St st for 40 rows. K and bind off.

Make clothes:

Pants—First side: Beg at waistline with green, cast on 26 sts. Work even in St st for 20 rows

(the knit side is the right side). *Next row:* Work across and inc 1 st at each end of row. Repeat last row once—30 sts (crotch). Work even for 8 rows. *Next row* (dec row): K and dec 1 st each end of row. Beg with P row, work 3 rows even in St st. Repeat dec row once—26 sts. Beg with P row work 5 rows even. K and bind off. **Second side:** Using dark blue, instead of green, make the same as the first side.

Finishing:

Body and Head: Holding the two body and head pieces together, wrong sides out, using matching yarns, sew together with back stitch, close along all edges except the bottom. Turn right side out. Stuff firmly. Sew bottom closed. **Face:** Using patterns, cut eyes out of navy felt, nose and mouth from red felt, and cheeks from pink felt. Using matching thread and back stitch, sew all in place on one side of head, placing a cheek piece right at each end of "turned-up" mouth. **Hair:** Wind orange yarn around a 9 in cardboard 20 times. Slip off cardboard carefully and tie around all strands tightly at center with another strand of yarn. Tie all strands together again about 1¼ in from each end of bundle. Do not cut loops at ends. Place bundle across top of head, along seam line, with middle tie at center of forehead, and, using matching thread, sew down to head at tied places. Back of head is left bare. **Arms:** Fold arm piece in half, wrong side out, and, with matching yarn, sew up around hand and up arm as for body and head piece, leaving top open. Turn right side out. Stuff firmly and fold flat at top with seam at underside of arm. Sew closed and sew in place on shoulders. **Legs:** Holding one first side and one second side of leg together, wrong sides out, with matching yarn sew around shoes and up front and back of stocking leg, leaving top edge open. Turn right side out. Stuff firmly, and fold flat across top, seam at front and back. Sew in place on lower edge of body, toes pointing to front. **Pants:** Holding the two pants pieces, with right sides together and using back stitch, sew center seam at front and back from waistline edge down to crotch. Refold to form legs, and sew inside leg seams. Turn right side out. Pull up over legs onto clown. For straps, cut two pieces of ribbon to fit from front waistline of pants, over shoulders, and down to back waistline, crossing in back. Sew in place, tucking ends inside pants top. Make a bow tie of ribbon and sew in place on front at top of shirt.

Make the smaller clown:

Make Body and Head (make two): Beg at lower edge of body with off-white and #4 needles, cast on 20 sts. Work even in St st for 34 rows. (The knit side is the right side.) **Shape Shoulders:** Bind off 5 sts at beg of next 2 rows—10 sts. Work even for 3 rows. *Next row:* P4, inc 1 st in next st, P5—11 sts. *Next row* **Head:** K and inc 1 st in each st across—22 sts. Beg with P row, work even in St st for 22 rows,

ending with a right side row. *Next row:* P across, dec 1 st at each end—20 sts. *Next row:* K2 tog across row—10 sts. *Next row:* P2 tog across row—5 sts. *Next row:* K2 tog, K1, K2 tog—3 sts. Cut yarn, leaving a long end for sewing. Thread yarn into yarn needle and pull through sts as you take them off knitting needle. **Arms** (make two): Beg at upper edge of arm, with off-white and #4 needles, cast on 14 sts. Work even in St st for 28 rows. *Next row* **Shape Hand:** K2 tog * K1, K2 tog, repeat from * across—9 sts. P 1 row. *Next row* (inc row): K1, * inc 1 st in next st, K1, repeat from * across row—13 sts. Beg with P row, work 6 rows even in St st. *Next row:* P2 tog across to last st, end P1—7 sts. K and bind off. **Legs** (make two): Beg at upper edge, with off-white and #4 needles, cast on 16 sts. Work even in St st for 32 rows. *Next row* (dec row): K1, * K2 tog, K1, repeat from * across row—11 sts. *Next row:* P5, P2 tog, P4—10 sts. Cut off-white, tie on blue and use to knit **Shoe** as follows: **First Side:** With blue, K across next row. *Next row:* P across 5 sts, put rem 5 sts onto holder for second side of shoe. *Next row:* Cast on 7 sts at beg of row, K across row—12 sts. Beg with P row, work 5 rows even in St st. K and bind off. **Second Side:** Put sts from holder onto needle with point at center front. Tie on blue and P across. K 1 row. *Next row:* Cast on 7 sts

at beg of row, P across row—12 sts. Work even in St st for 5 rows. P and bind off.

Make clothes:

Pants: (make two alike): Beg at waistline edge, with #6 needles and variegated yarn, cast on 22 sts. Work even in St st for 6 rows (the purl side is the right side). *Next row:* K6, inc 1 st in each of next 10 sts, K6—32 sts. Beg with P row, work even in St st for 7 rows. *Next row:* K12 sts, inc 1 st in each of next 8 sts, K12—40 sts. P 1 row. *Next row:* K and inc 1 st at beg and end of row. P 1 row. Repeat last 2 rows once—44 sts (crotch). *Next row:* (dec row): K and dec 1 st at beg and end of row. P 1 row, K 1 row, P 1 row. *Next row:* Repeat dec row once—40 sts. Beg with P row, work St st even for 5 rows. *Next row:* K12, K2 tog (8 times), K12—32 sts. Beg with P row, work 13 rows even. *Next row:* K6, K2 tog (10 times) K6—22 sts. Beg with P row work even for 3 rows. K and bind off. **Hat:** This is made in one piece knitted sideways and sewn up with a seam in back. With #6 needles and blue, cast on 17 sts. *Row 1:* K across row. *Row 2:* (right side): K10, P7. Repeat these 2 rows for a total of 56 rows. K and bind off.

Finishing:

Body and Head: Sew together, stuff, and sew closed same as for the larger clown. **Face:** Using patterns, cut eyes from blue felt and nose and mouth from red felt.

Sew in place as for larger clown, omitting cheek pieces. Hat is finished next and sewn onto head, then hair is made and sewn on around head under brim of hat. **Hat:** Using matching thread and overcast stitch on wrong side of work, sew bound-off row to cast-on row to form seam for back of hat. Run a piece of yarn in and out along garter stitch edge and pull up to gather together for top of hat. Pull tight and fasten securely on wrong side. Turn right-side-out and allow the St st edge to roll up for brim. Sew a pom-pom to top of hat. Place hat on head and sew securely in place. **Hair:** Wind orange yarn around 3 fingers 15 times. Slip off carefully and tie around bundle at center with another length of yarn. Repeat 5 times to make a total of six bundles. Sew one bundle at each side of face, just under hat brim. Fill in with the remaining four around back of head to make a complete line of hair just under the hat brim. Trim loose ends of yarn, but do not cut loops. **Arms:** Sew up, stuff and sew onto clown as for larger clown. **Legs:** Fold and sew as for arms, sewing sides of shoes together down around front, across bottom and up back.

Sew back seam, leaving top open. Turn right side out. Stuff firmly and sew closed straight across top with toes to front. Sew in place at bottom of body.

Make clothes:

Pants: Using matching yarn, sew together as for the larger clown's pants. Turn right side out and put on clown, omitting straps. **Shirt:** Front: Holding one 3 in by 5 in piece of orange felt and one 3 in by 5 in piece of yellow felt together for front of shirt, seam them together along one 5 in side, with a ¼ in seam. This is the center front seam. **Back:** The other 3 in by 5 in pieces of orange and yellow felt are for the back of the shirt, but do not sew together as for front. Instead, hold one side of the orange piece against the right side of the front yellow piece and seam them together along one 3 in side of the pieces, sewing in from the outer edge toward center front seam for ¾ in only—this is a shoulder seam. Repeat last step for second side, seaming the yellow back piece to orange front piece at shoulder. Pin center back together, wrong side out. Do not sew yet. Colors should be just op-

posite to the front colors. Keep front and back felt together. **Sleeves:** Place the 5 in (longer) side of the orange piece against one outer edge of the front and back pieces of shirt (right sides together) and center at shoulder. Sew in place with ¼ in seam for first sleeve. Repeat on other outer edge of front and back piece with remaining yellow piece for second sleeve. Remember the 5 in side is the armhole side and the 3½ in side is the length of the sleeve. Sew ¼ in seams at sides and underarm of sleeve, on wrong side, clipping carefully on curves. Unpin and turn right side out. **Neckline Facing:** Fold felt to inside around neckline, tapering from a ½ in turn down at center back to ⅛ in at shoulder, down to ½ in at center front, back to ⅛ in at second shoulder and then to ½ in again when returning to back. Sew down in place. **To Trim:** Gather the ruffled trim to fit around the neckline and sew in place. Sew on four pom-poms evenly spaced along front seam and one on the top side of wrist edge of each sleeve. Place shirt on clown, with opening at back. Overcast opening closed for center back seam.

Patterns for Two Clowns

For larger clown:

Eye	Nose	Cheek	Mouth

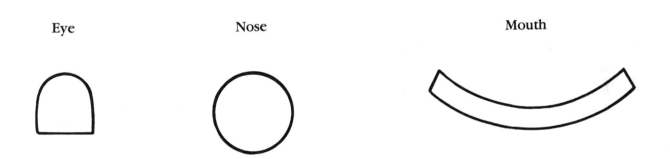

For smaller clown:

Eye	Nose	Mouth

Racquel Raccoon

All raccoons wear cute little masks but not all wear such pretty little dresses as this one does. Because she is very much a little lady in her "patchwork" dress and matching bow, I have named her Racquel.

Her features, including the face "mask," are cut from felt and appliquéd on (or they could be glued in place). In addition, like all raccoons, she has a pretty striped tail. She is 15 inches tall.

To make Racquel Raccoon you will need:

Bulky weight acrylic yarn:
    4 oz brown tweed
    ½ oz white
    ½ oz black
OR, approximately the same amount of knitting worsted weight yarn.
Fabric: small amounts of each of a red print, white print, and blue print (for patchwork dress)
OR, a 20½ × 3½ in piece (for plain dress)
20½ in iron-on hem tape, red or to match the dress fabric
30 in of 1-inch-wide bias tape, red or to match dress fabric (for waistband and shoulder straps)
16 in of ¾-in grosgrain ribbon in red or color of your choice for head bow
Small amounts of black and white felt
Sewing thread to match felt, fabrics, and ribbon
1 pair #6 knitting needles
Yarn needle
Sewing needle
Polyester fiberfill

White glue—if you plan to use it

Racquel Raccoon's body and head are made in one piece, sewn up the back, shaped, and stuffed like the bears'. In the same manner, her arms, legs, nose, and ears are knit separately and sewn onto the body. She is knit using a bulky yarn, which makes the work go very fast. You can also use knitting worsted weight yarn—doubled—and get the same results. The dress she is wearing is indeed made up of patchwork with an appliquéd heart on the bib top. I think the special dress is well worth the time spent, but if patchwork isn't fun for you, Racquel would be just about as cute in a dress made from a single-colored print or a solid color—even with just a bow around her neck! (The measurements for making a plain dress are included here.)

Make Racquel Raccoon:

Starting at lower edge of body with brown tweed, cast on 40 sts. Work even in St st for 30 rows (K side is right side). *Next row* (inc row): *K1, inc 1 st in next st, repeat from * across row—60 sts. **Head:** Beg with P row, work even in St st on these 60 sts for 26 rows. *Next row:* P2 tog across—30 sts. K and bind off. **Arms** (make two): Using brown tweed, cast on 20 sts. Work even in St st for 14 rows. *Next row:* K2 tog across—10 sts. P 1 row. *Complete as follows:* Clip yarn, leaving a long end for sewing. Thread yarn into needle and pull through sts as you take them off knitting needle. **Legs** (make two): With brown tweed, cast on 20 sts. Work even in St st for 22 rows. *Next row:* K2 tog across—10 sts. P 1 row. Complete as for arms. **Ears** (make four alike—two using tweed yarn and two using white yarn): Starting at lower edge, cast on 12 sts. K 1 row. P 1 row. *Next row:* K and dec 1 st each end of

row. P 1 row. Repeat last 2 rows until 4 sts remain, ending with P row. *Next row:* K and bind off, leaving yarn end. Thread this end into yarn needle and sew down to edge of ear. Hide end on wrong side and clip off. **Nose:** Using white, cast on 28 sts. Work even in St st for 8 rows. *Next row:* K2 tog across—14 sts. Complete as for arms. **Tail:** Using black and starting at upper edge, cast on 14 sts. K 1 row. P 1 row. Drop black, but do not cut. Tie on brown tweed and use to K 1 row, then P 1 row. Carrying color not in use up side of work, repeat last 4 rows 5 times more for a total of 24 rows. *Next row:* using black, K 2 tog across—7 sts. P 1 row with black. *Next row:* Continuing to use black alone, K2 tog across to last st, K1—4 sts. P 1 row. Complete as for arms.

Finishing:

Body and Head: Bring sides of body and head piece together to form a tube with right side (knit side) out. Using matching yarn in yarn needle, overcast side edges together, working on right side. Fold piece flat with seam at center back and sew closed across top of head with overcast stitch. Stuff firmly. Sew closed across bottom edge. *To Form Neckline:* Thread a long length of matching yarn into yarn needle. Working on inc row, take a few stitches to secure yarn at back seam. Wrap yarn around raccoon twice, pulling hard to pull piece in to form neck. Holding firmly, return to where yarn was first secured, and secure again with sev-

eral stitches. Run needle along under work for a couple of inches, return to surface, and clip yarn off close, being careful not to cut raccoon. **Arms:** Thread yarn that was pulled through last stitches of arm into yarn needle. Pull up tight, bringing sides together and forming a tube (right side out). Fasten securely. Take a few stitches to close lower end completely. Using matching yarn, overcast side edges together. Stuff firmly. Fold upper edge together with seam at one side and sew closed straight across top. Sew arms in place at sides of body, with seams at underside. **Legs:** Finish in same manner as for arms. Sew in place on lower edge of body with seams at inner sides of legs. **Ears:** Holding one tweed piece and one white piece together for each ear with right sides out, and using tweed yarn, overcast the upper edges together. Do not overcast bottom edge. Do not stuff. Sew in place on sides of head at the ends of top seam with white side facing front. (Tweed side is back side of ear.) **Nose:** Thread yarn that was pulled through last stitches of nose into yarn needle. Pull up tightly to gather and fasten, taking a few stitches to close end of nose completely. On right side, overcast seam formed by pulling sides of piece together. Stuff firmly. Sew in place on face, with seam at underside. **Tail:** Thread yarn that was pulled through last stitches of tail into yarn needle. Pull tight and fasten. Form piece into tube shape right side out as for arms and legs and sew up seam. Stuff—but not quite as firmly as for arms and legs. Gather upper edge, pull up to fasten and sew closed. Sew tail in place on back of raccoon with seam at underside. **Face:** Trace patterns and use to cut upper mask piece from white felt and lower mask piece from black felt. Cut outer eye from white felt and inner eye from black felt. Using matching thread and back stitch, sew all in place on face, tucking white mask pieces down in back of black mask pieces for ½ in. If you'd rather, you can glue the mask pieces and eyes in place instead of sewing. Cut nose tip from black felt and sew or glue in place on nose.

Make clothes:

Patchwork Dress: Use patterns to cut five large pieces from blue print and five large pieces from red print. Cut ten small pieces from red print and ten small pieces from white print (¼ in seams are already allowed on all pieces). Sew the larger pieces together in a row, alternating the blue and red prints. Sew the smaller pieces together in a row, alternating the red and white prints. Next seam together one long edge of the first piece (the larger—blue and red) and one long edge of the second piece (the smaller—red and white) to form one 3½ × 20½ in piece. Turn ¼ in up to wrong side on one long edge of red and white prints. Cover with hem tape and iron in place. Seam the two short sides together for back seam. Run a thread around top edge (blue and red prints). Slip skirt on body by pulling up over legs. Pull up thread to gather tightly around waistline. Sew in place by sewing right through onto raccoon body. Using pattern for bib, cut two pieces alike from white print. Holding rights sides together, sew pieces together with ¼ in seams along two sides and across top. Leave lower edge open. Trim seams and turn to right side. Place bib piece on front with lower edge right above top edge of skirt piece. Sew in place by sewing just along lower edge. Measure and cut a piece of bias binding to fit around waistline, plus a little for fold-over at end. Place around waist tightly, covering stitching at top of skirt and bottom of bib piece. Fold end over in back and sew in place, taking a few stitches through to raccoon to secure. Measure a piece of bias for each shoulder strap to fit from under bib in front, cross in back, and extend under waistband in back. Sew in place. Using patterns, cut larger heart from red print and smaller heart from blue print. Appliqué blue heart onto red heart, then appliqué red heart onto bib front with point of heart extending down over waistband. Tie grosgrain ribbon into bow and, with matching thread, sew in place on top of head between ears.

To make plain dress instead of patchwork:

Cut a piece of fabric 3½ × 20½ in for skirt and use pattern for bib as before. Now make and sew on dress in same manner as for patchwork dress. Add heart appliqué or not as you wish.

Patterns for Racquel Raccoon

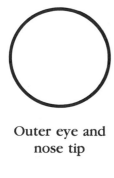

Outer eye and
nose tip

Inner eye

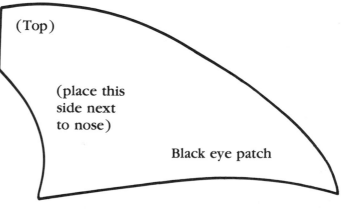

(Top)

(place this side next to nose)

Black eye patch

(reverse for second side)

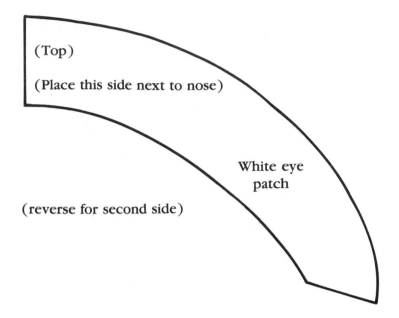

(Top)

(Place this side next to nose)

(reverse for second side)

White eye
patch

Small heart
appliqué

Large patch (for dress)

Large heart
appliqué

Small patch
(for dress)

(Top)

Bib

(cut 2)

Two Nice Mice

Do you like mice? Here are two that are so cute and cuddly that they appeal to everyone. Their small size makes them just right for everyone to hold, including babies: 4 to 4½ inches long and 2½ to 3 inches high, depending on the yarn they are made from.

These Nice Mice are not only fun as playthings but can be used as decorations as well. How about several Christmas mice to set on your mantel or hang on your tree? Try some with hearts for Valentines or flowers for birthdays. They can decorate the outside of packages also. After the gift is opened, there is an extra gift of a little toy to love. Remember, pastels are always good, but babies and children love bright colors, too, so use up your pretty scraps.

To make the House Mouse you'll need:

Acrylic yarn of knitting worsted
    weight:
    1 oz gray
    Very small amounts of 3 different shades of pink
    Very small amount of black
1 pair #4 knitting needles
Yarn needle
Polyester fiberfill

To make the Christmas Mouse you'll need:

Acrylic yarn of knitting worsted
    weight:
    1 oz white
    Very small amount of black
Felt: very small amounts of red and green
1 pair #4 knitting needles
Yarn needle
Sewing thread to match felt [OR white glue]
Sewing needle
Polyester fiberfill

The mice are extra-easy: just three pieces exactly alike for the bodies and then two ears, all done in easy garter stitch. Both are made of knitting worsted weight yarn, but some brands seem to knit up a little bigger than others. That really doesn't matter here—any of the knitting worsteds will make up into a loveable sized mouse. The three body pieces are sewn together and stuffed, the ears are sewn on, and the eyes and nose are embroidered. The tails are twisted cords of yarn (or could be crocheted or braided of yarn instead). Then they can be decorated however you wish. I have made a gray "house" mouse and a white "Christmas" mouse. My House Mouse wears just a pink yarn bow above his ears to match his eyes and tail, but the Christmas Mouse has pretty green holly

leaves and red berries of felt on his sides (glued or appliquéd on), and a red bow at the end of his tail.

Make the House Mouse:

Body (make three): With gray, beginning at tail end, cast on 2 sts. K 1 row. *Next row:* K and inc 1 st in each st. K 1 row even. *Next row* (inc row): K and inc 1 st in first and last st. K 1 row even. Repeat last 2 rows until there are 16 sts on needle, ending with inc row. Work even in garter st (K each row) for 16 rows. *Next row* (dec row): K and dec 1 st at each end of row. K 3 rows even. Repeat last 4 rows until 2 sts remain, ending with dec row, but do not knit the 3 rows even after working row that decreases to 2 sts. K and bind off, leaving long ends for sewing together. Bound-off sts are at nose end of mouse. **Ears** (make two): With gray, starting at lower edge of ear, cast on 8 sts.

Work even in garter st for 6 rows. *Next row:* Slip 1, K1, pass the slip st over the K st, K to last 2 sts, K2 tog—6 sts. K 1 row even. Repeat last 2 rows once—4 sts. K and bind off, leaving 6 in end of yarn. Sew this end down to top of ear, rounding edge as you do so. Run in and hide end along one edge of ear.

Finishing:

Body: Hold two body pieces together and sew together along one side from nose end to tail end, using a back stitch and forming a seam ¼ in or so in from edge. This forms top of mouse. For bottom of mouse, separate the unsewn edges and insert the third body piece between them, matching edges on each side. Sew together along one edge with back stitch and ¼ in seam as for top, sewing from nose to tail and leaving 1 in or so unsewn for turning. Do not cut yarn yet: leave it to sew closed later. Repeat for second edge. Turn to right side (seams are now on inside). Stuff,

but not too firmly. Using yarn that was left hanging, sew opening closed at tail end. **Ears:** Using matching yarn, sew lower edge of ears in place on sides of body about one third of the way back from nose end. **Face:** Thread yarn needle with light pink yarn and use to embroider one eye, high on "head" just in front of one ear. Do not cut yarn, but pull needle with yarn through to other side of "head" and pull in a little to indent first eye. Secure, then embroider second eye. Then pull back through to first side to indent second eye, and secure by first eye. Using black, embroider nose at very front end of mouse. **Tail:** Make a tail 6½ in long, using three shades of pink yarn, twisted into a cord, crocheted or braided together. *To make bow:* Thread two 18 in long strands of pink yarn into yarn needle together. Pull needle through top of mouse just under top seam and just behind ears. Pull yarn up to be equal on both sides, remove needle and tie firmly into a bow. Trim ends if necessary.

Make the Christmas Mouse:

Body: With white yarn, follow directions for knitting the three body pieces and two ears, in same manner as for House Mouse.

Finishing:

Body and Head: Sew together, stuff, and sew on ears as for the House Mouse. Use black to embroider both the eyes and nose in the same manner as for the House Mouse. Use white to make a 6½-in tail of twisted cord or crochet or braid yarn. Cut a piece of red felt ¼ in wide and 6 in long. Tie into a bow at the end of the tail. Trim ends. A narrow ribbon may be used instead, if you wish. **Decorations:** Trace patterns and use to cut four holly leaves from green felt and six berries from red felt. Sew (or glue) two leaves with three berries at center between them on each side of mouse.

Patterns for Christmas Mouse

Holly leaf

Holly berry

Benjamin Bear

Although this bear is a much bigger bear than the ones described earlier and has a personality all his own, you might want to make him as a big brother to one of the smaller ones. He sits about 12 inches high. I've named him Benjamin but like to call him "Big Ben" for fun.

Like the other bears, this larger bear can be made with different colors and dressed differently for variety. How about using pink bows or ruffles and lace to make a girl bear?

To make Benjamin Bear, you'll need:

Acrylic yarn of knitting worsted
    weight: 4½ oz medium
    brown
24 in of 1½-inch wide braid
Felt:
    8 × 9 in piece of turquoise
    (for vest)
    Small piece of orange (for vest
    pockets)
    Small pieces of white, tur-
    quoise, black, and red (for
    features)
Embroidery floss: small amount
    of black
1 pair #4 knitting needles
Yarn needle
White glue
Sewing thread to match felt for
    vest and tongue, and braid
Sewing needle
Polyester fiberfill

He is knitted and stuffed in the same way as the smaller bears. The body and head are knitted in one piece, sewn up the back, stuffed, and shaped. The arms, legs, ears, and nose are knitted separately, stuffed, and then sewn onto the body. His eyes and nose are cut from felt and can be appliquéd in place (or glued on, as I have done). His tongue, also felt, is sewn on just below the line embroidered for his mouth. An extra cute addition is the paw pads on the bottom of the feet. They too I have cut from felt and glued on. He is dressed in a felt vest with contrasting-color pockets put on with top stitching, and he has a big bow tied around his neck.

Make Benjamin Bear:

Body and Head: Starting at lower edge of body, cast on 60 sts. Work even in St st for 48 rows. (The purl side of all pieces is the right side). *Next row* (inc row): * K1, inc 1 st in next st, repeat from * across row—90 sts. **Head:** Next row: Beg with P row, work even in St st for 39 rows. *Next row:* K2 tog across—45 sts. Purl and bind off. **Arms** (make two): Cast on 30 sts. Work even in St st for 27 rows. *Next row:* P2 tog across—15 sts. *Next row:* K2 tog across to last st, K1—8 sts. Clip yarn, leaving a long end. Thread yarn into a yarn needle and pull through the sts while taking them off the knitting needle. Do not cut yet. Instead, leave it to be used later for sewing seam and sewing onto body. **Legs** (make two): Cast on 30 sts. Work even in St st for 18 rows. *Next row* (for foot): K9, inc 1 st in each of next 12 sts, K9—42 sts. P 1 row. *Next row:* K15, inc 1 st in each of next 12 sts, K 15—54 sts. Beg with P row, work even for 8 rows. *Next row:* P 2 tog across—27 sts.

K and bind off. **Nose:** Cast on 42 sts. Work in St st for 11 rows. *Next row:* P 2 tog across—21 sts. *Next row:* K2 tog across to last st, K1—11 sts. Cut yarn, leaving a long end, and finish as for arms. **Ears** (make four pieces—two for each ear): Cast on 18 sts. Work even in St st for 9 rows (ending with K row). *Next row:* Work across and dec 1 st each end of row. Repeat last row 7 times more—2 sts. Cut yarn, leaving long end. Thread into needle and pull through sts as you take them off the knitting needle. Sew these sts down firmly to top of ear piece, thereby rounding the top of the ear. Run in end on wrong side and clip off.

Finishing:

Body and Head: Bring sides of body and head piece together to form a tube with wrong side (knit side) out. Using yarn needle and matching yarn, overcast side edges together. Fold piece flat with seam at center back and sew closed across top of head. Turn to right side. Stuff firmly. Sew closed across bottom edge. **To Form Neckline:** Thread a long length of yarn into yarn needle. Working on inc row, take a few stitches to secure yarn at back seam. Wrap yarn around bear twice, pulling hard to pull piece in to form neck. Holding firmly, return to where yarn was first secured, and secure again with several stitches. Run needle along under work for a couple of inches, return to surface and clip yarn off close, being careful not to cut into bear. **Arms:** Thread yarn that was pulled

through last stitches of arm into yarn needle. Pull up tight, bringing sides together wrong side out and forming a tube. Fasten securely. Take a few stitches to close lower end completely. Using matching yarn, overcast side edges together. Turn to right side. Stuff firmly. Run a matching yarn around upper edge, pull up to gather together, and sew closed. Sew arms in place at sides of body, facing a little forward, with seams at underside. **Legs:** Fold leg piece flat wrong side out with inc part (toe) on one side and edges together on the other side. Overcast seam across bottom of foot and up the side. Turn right side out. Stuff, pushing out increased part to form toe. Run a matching yarn around top, gather to close and secure. Sew in place on lower front body with toes facing forward and up so bear can sit up. **Ears:** Place two ear pieces together wrong side out and overcast edges together, working around curved edges only, *twice* to make it firm. Do not overcast bottom edge. Do not stuff. Turn right side out. Sew in place on sides of head at the ends of top seam. **Nose:** Thread yarn that was pulled through last stitches of nose into yarn needle. Pull up tightly to gather and fasten, taking a few stitches to close end of nose completely. On wrong side, overcast seam formed by pulling sides of piece together. Turn right side out. Stuff firmly. Sew in place on face, with seam at underside. Trace patterns and use to cut outer eyes from white felt, inner eyes and vest back and front pieces from turquoise felt and tongue from red felt. Cut nose tip and paw pad pieces from black felt and pockets from orange felt. Glue inner eyes on outer eyes and glue in place on face. Glue nose tip in place and paw pads onto bottom of feet, placing the three small "toes" above the larger pad. Using six strands of embroidery floss, embroider a line down from nose tip and along straight under this for mouth. Using matching thread, sew tongue in place right under mouth line, sewing only the upper edge of tongue to bear. Allow lower edge to hang free. Eyes, nose tip and paw pads can all be appliquéd in place with matching thread instead of gluing, if you wish.

Make vest:

With matching thread, sew front vest pieces to back piece at shoulders and sides, taking ¼ in seams. Turn to right side and sew pockets in place on each side of front, using contrasting thread and top stitching. Cut braid to fit around neck and sew in place. Form remaining braid into a large bow and sew in place under chin, allowing loops to hang down.

Patterns for Benjamin Bear

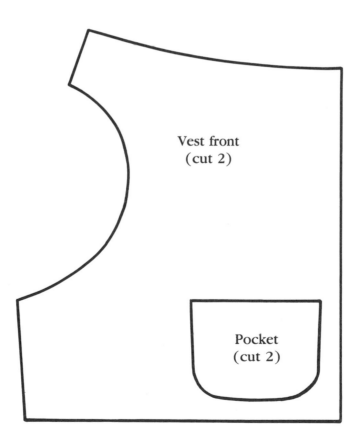

Vest front
(cut 2)

Pocket
(cut 2)

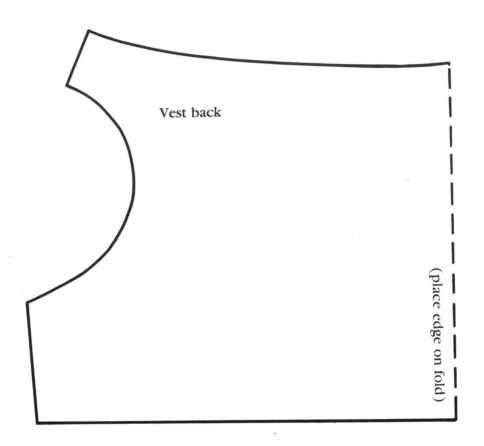

Vest back

(place edge on fold)

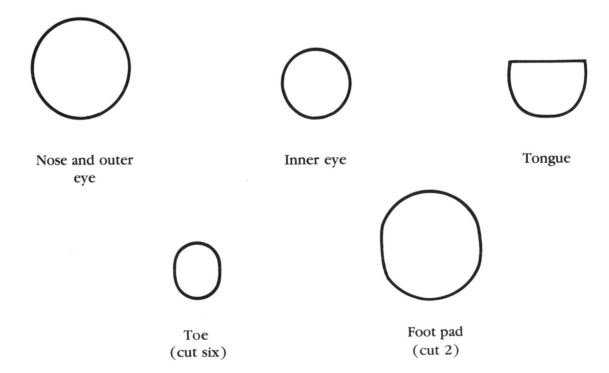

Nose and outer
eye

Inner eye

Tongue

Toe
(cut six)

Foot pad
(cut 2)

Baby Bunting
in a Basket

This baby is not only snug in a bunting, but has a little lined basket to be carried about in. The baby and bunting are worked together in one unit, then the hood, then the basket. Afterwards, the handles are crocheted and added, and the basket is lined with a pretty print. The baby in the bunting is about 9½ inches long, and the basket is about 12 inches long—just the right size to be carried easily and loved by any little girl.

To make Baby Bunting you'll need:

Acrylic yarn of knitting worsted weight:
   1 oz medium blue
   ½ oz pink
   Very small amount of yellow (for hair)
9½ in of ¾-inch white eyelet ruffle
28 in of ¾-inch pink flowered braid
Felt: very small amount of medium blue (for eyes)
Embroidery floss: small amounts of red and brown
1 pair #4 knitting needles
Yarn needle
Sewing thread to match felt, braid, and hair
Sewing needle
Polyester fiberfill
Red colored pencil

To make the basket you'll need:

Acrylic yarn of knitting worsted weight: 4½ oz light brown

⅓ yard of yellow "baby" print
   quilted fabric
1 pair #6 knitting needles
1 size G crochet hook
Yarn needle
Sewing thread to match fabric
Sewing needle
Note: Double strand of yarn is
   used to work basket.

Knit the baby and bunting alike, starting at the bottom with blue for the bunting and continuing on to the top part with pink for the head. These are then sewn together to form the front and back of Baby Bunting. The hood is knit separately in one piece and sewn onto the head after Baby Bunting is assembled and stuffed. After the face is added, a pretty ruffle and colorful braid are sewn around the front of the hood. Braid is also added to the front of the bunting and around the neckline. A few yellow yarn curls are tucked under the hood at the forehead and sewn in place.

Knit the basket in three pieces—one forms the two long sides and the bottom, and the other two pieces form the ends. A basket-stitch pattern is used, which is simple to do because it is made up only of knit and purl stitches. After the three pieces are worked, they are sewn together to form an oblong basket. Three rows of single crochet are then worked around the top edge to make it firm and pull it into shape. I have used a quilted baby print to line the basket, but almost any fabric is suitable.

Make Baby Bunting:

Body (Make two): With blue, beg at lower edge of bunting, cast on 26 sts. Work even in St st for 8 rows. (The knit side is the right side). *Next row:* K and dec 1 st at each end of row—24 sts. Beg with P row, work even for 9 rows. *Next row:* K and dec 1 st at each end of row—22 sts. Beg with P row, work even in St st for 32 rows, ending with right side row. *Next row:* P2 tog across row—11 sts. **Head:** Cut blue, tie on pink and use to K 1 row, P 1 row. *Next row:* K and inc 1 st in each st across—22 sts. Beg with P row, work even in St st for 22 rows, ending with K row. P 1 row, dec 1 st at each end of row—20 sts. Dec for top of head: *Row 1:* K2 tog across row—10 sts. *Row 2:* P2 tog across row—5 sts. *Row 3:* K2 tog, K1, K2 tog—3 sts. Cut yarn, leaving long end for sewing together. Thread yarn into yarn needle, and pull through sts as you take them off the knitting needle. Pull up tight and fasten securely, but do not cut. **Hood:** Using blue, beg at face edge, cast on 48 sts. Work even in St st for 22 rows, ending with P row. (The knit side is the right side.) Dec for back of hood: K 10; K2 tog 14 times, K 10—34 sts. *Next row:* P and bind off tightly. Cut yarn, leaving long end for sewing back seam.

Finishing:

Body: Holding the two bunting/ body pieces with right sides together, sew together with matching yarn and back stitch close

along outside edge, leaving 2 in open at top of head. Turn to right side. Stuff firmly and sew top of head closed. **To Shape Hood:** Fold hood piece so that side edges of work are together with right (knit) side inside. Sew the bound-off edge together, using matching yarn and overcast stitch, to form a back seam on hood. Place on head, with seam down center back of head. Sew in place on doll along bottom at neckline. **Face:** Using two strands of red embroidery floss, embroider nose and mouth in outline stitch. Using pattern, cut eyes from blue felt and sew in place with matching thread and back stitch. (These can be glued on with white glue, if you'd rather do so.) Using two strands of brown floss and outline stitch, embroider heavy brown lines for eyebrows right at top of eyes. Rub red pencil lightly on face to make pink cheeks. Wind yellow yarn around one finger 10 times. Slip off carefully and tie loops together at one end with another short piece of yarn. Tuck this tied end under hood at top of forehead, and sew all loops in place with matching thread to form curls. Trim ends. **To Complete Hood:** Place eyelet ruffle (to extend forward) around face edge of hood. Measure and cut a piece of braid to fit around same edge. Place on top of eyelet edge and sew all together around hood, taking a few stitches down through hood to head to secure all in place. Measure and cut a piece of braid to fit from under chin, down front of bunting for 4½ in, fold to form point and back up again to under chin. Sew in place. Measure and cut a piece of braid to fit around neck, plus ½ in or so for overlap at back. Sew in place, covering all other ends of ruffle and braid.

Make the basket:

To Make Ends Of Basket (Make two): Using double strand of yarn, cast on 21 sts. Work in pattern as follows: *Row 1* (right side): Knit. *Row 2:* K5, *P3, K5, repeat from * across row. *Row 3:* P5 *K3, P5, repeat from * across row. *Row 4:* Repeat Row 2. *Row 5:* Knit. *Row 6:* K1 *P3, K5; repeat from *, end last repeat K1, instead of K5. *Row 7:* P1 *K3, P5, repeat from *, end last repeat P1 instead of P5. *Row 8:* Repeat Row 6. Work rows 1 through 8 then repeat rows 1 through 4 only. *Next row:* K and bind off. **To Make Long Sides and Bottom** (one piece): Using double strand of yarn, cast on 45 sts and work in same pattern as for ends. Continue work until pattern has been completed 7 times—a total of 56 rows. *Next row:* K and bind off.

Finishing:

Using a single strand of yarn and referring to diagram for placement, sew a short end (using overcast stitch on wrong side) onto each side edge of large piece, spacing an equal distance between top and bottom, as shown. Be sure all right sides are facing the same way. Now, before completing basket, measure for lining by placing the flat basket piece on lining fabric. Pin in place, and cut around all edges, adding ½ in for seams. Unpin, lay lining aside, and continue to sew basket together. At one corner, bring the two sides marked A together and overcast together with single strand on wrong side. Repeat in same manner for the other three corners. Turn basket to right side. Using crochet hook and double strand of yarn, work single crochet around all edges of basket for 3 rows, decreasing as necessary to pull this top edge in to form a nice "basket" shape—about 27 in to 28 in around top. **Make Straps For Handles** (make two): Using double strand of yarn, single crochet a chain 10½ in long, then work one single crochet in each single crochet along chain. Sew one strap onto each long side of basket, placing ends about 4 in apart on outside edge. **Line Basket:** Bring corners of lining fabric up together as for basket. Sew together taking ½ in seams on wrong side. Place lining into basket, wrong sides together. Turn raw edge to inside, about ½ in down from top edge of basket and sew in place.

Patterns for Baby Bunting in a Basket

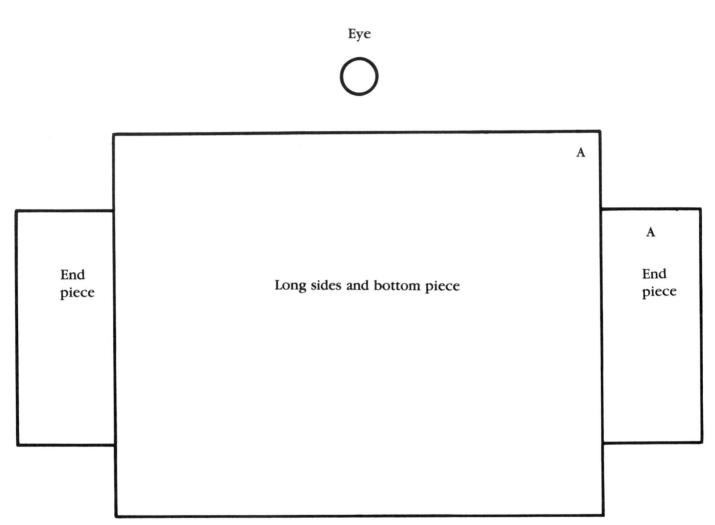

Eye

End
piece

Long sides and bottom piece

A

A

End
piece

Diagram for Placement of Basket Pieces

Roly-Poly Family

Mr. and Mrs. Roly-Poly and their baby are three funny, clown-like characters, who (just as their name implies) are great to toss or roll about. They are made of colorful yarns and trimmed with bright pieces of felt. Any colors of yarn and felt you have can be used to make them. They are an attractive way to use up scraps, since they are "fun to look at and play with" toys. Father Roly-Poly is 7 inches tall, Mother Roly-Poly is 6¼ inches tall, and Baby is 4¼ inches tall.

To make Father Roly-Poly you'll need:

Acrylic yarn of knitting worsted weight:
   1¼ oz variegated pink
   Small amount of dark brown (for hair)
Felt: small amounts of white, blue, orange, pink, yellow, and red
2 medium size moving eyes
Embroidery floss: small amount of red
1 pair #4 knitting needles
Yarn needle
Sewing thread to sew on eyes and to match felt pieces if you plan to sew them on instead of gluing them
Sewing needle
Polyester fiberfill
White glue
6½ in long piece of cardboard

To make Mother Roly-Poly you'll need:

Acrylic yarn of knitting worsted weight:
   ½ oz variegated pink
   ½ oz solid pink

Small amount of yellow (for hair)
Felt: small amounts of turquoise, pink, white, and red
2 medium size moving eyes
Embroidery floss: small amount of red
1 pair #4 knitting needles
Yarn needle
Sewing thread to sew on eyes and to match felt pieces if you plan to sew them on instead of gluing them
Sewing needle
Polyester fiberfill
White glue
6½ in long piece of cardboard

To make Baby Roly-Poly you'll need:

Acrylic yarn of knitting worsted weight:
   ½ oz pink
   Small amount of medium brown (for hair)
Felt: small amounts of purple, white, yellow, and orange
2 small size moving eyes
Embroidery floss: small amount of red
1 pair #4 knitting needles

Yarn needle
Sewing thread to sew on eyes and to match felt pieces if you plan to sew them on instead of gluing them
Sewing needle
Polyester fiberfill
White glue
4¼ in long piece of cardboard

Each Roly-Poly is extra-simple to make and can be done very quickly. They are all made in the same way, by knitting one oblong piece using easy garter stitch. The ends of this piece are sewn together to form a back seam, the bottom is gathered and closed and after it is stuffed, the top is gathered and closed. The head and body shape is made by pulling and fastening a yarn tightly around this oblong stuffed shape. Their faces are made by embroidering on the mouth and nose and sewing on moving eyes (the eyes can be made of felt or embroidered on for very small children). Their hair is made of yarn and glued on. The hands, arms and all decorations are made of felt and glued on also. Father wears a collar and a tie trimmed with a small flower, and

Mother wears a collar with a flower trim. Baby also has a collar with flower trim and wears a little flower in her hair. All three have flowers covering the gathering stitches at the bottom end. Use up the yarns you have left from other projects to make these, tie on more of another color if you run out, use any colors of felt. You'll end up with a funny, unique Roly-Poly.

Make Father Roly-Poly:

Body: Using variegated pink yarn, cast on 36 sts. *Row 1:* slip first st as if to K, but move it to right-hand needle (this makes a knotted edge), K across row. Repeat this row until piece measures 9 in from beg. **Note:** Do not stretch piece when measuring. Bind off loosely, leaving long end for sewing.

Finishing:

Fold over piece so bound-off edge and cast-on edge meet. Using overcast stitch, sew these edges together to form a back seam. Run a matching yarn around through knotted stitches on one edge. Pull up tight, fasten securely and take a few stitches across the small opening that is left to close it completely, for bottom of toy. Turn inside out. Stuff firmly. Gather top and close as for bottom. Measure length of toy and, on back seam, mark a point halfway between top and bottom. The dividing line between the body and head is made ½ in above this mark. To divide the body and head, thread a long length of matching yarn into yarn needle. Take a few stitches on the back seam ½ in above the marker, wind yarn around toy twice, and pull in hard to separate body from

head. Return needle and yarn to starting point, and take several stitches to secure again. Run yarn in under work for a little way, return to surface and clip off, being careful not to cut toy.

To make hair, wind dark brown yarn around the 6½ in piece of cardboard 20 times. Slip off cardboard carefully and tie around bunch at center with a 12 in length of yarn. Cut all loops at each end of bunch. Thread one end of tying yarn into needle and use to secure the hair to center top of head. Arrange hair evenly around head, leaving space for face at front. Trim ends as you wish (I think an uneven look is the cutest). Carefully lift a section at a time, spread glue on head and press hair back in place. To embroider the mouth and nose, use six strands of red floss, outline stitch for the mouth and satin stitch for the nose. Sew the moving eyes on securely (or make eyes from felt and sew on, or embroider on). Using patterns, cut arms and large flower center from orange felt, hands from pink felt and tie and large flower for bottom end from blue felt. For collar, measure around neck and cut a piece of ¾-inch wide white felt to fit. Cut a small flower for trim on tie from yellow felt and center from red felt. It may be easier to cut these freehand. Glue all in place (or sew on if you wish).

Make Mother Roly-Poly:

Body: Using variegated yarn, cast on 32 sts. *Row 1:* Slip first st as if to K, but move onto right-hand needle (this makes a knotted edge), K across. Repeat this row until piece measures 1 in from beg. **Note:** Do not stretch piece when measuring. Cut variegated, tie on solid pink and use to work for 1 in more. Cut solid pink, tie on variegated again and use to work for 1 in. Continue in this manner, alternating the variegated and solid yarn every inch until piece measures a total of 8 in from beg, ending with solid pink. Bind off loosely, leaving a long end for sewing.

Finishing:

Sew together, stuff and finish as for Father Roly-Poly, running in all ends through top of stitches on one side (wrong side) before turning right-side-out. Make dividing line for body and head ¼ in above the halfway mark between top and bottom. Using yellow yarn, make hair same as for Father Roly-Poly, but do not cut loops. Sew to top of head, arrange and glue in place in same manner. Make face same as for Father Roly-Poly. Using patterns, cut arms from turquoise felt, hands from pink felt, flowers for collar trim and bottom from red felt and flower center for bottom from white felt. To make center for flower on collar simply cut a very small diamond shape from white felt. Measure around neck and cut collar from ½ in wide turquoise felt to fit. Glue or sew all in place.

Make Baby Roly-Poly:

Body: Using pink yarn, cast on 20 sts. Work same as for Father Roly-Poly until piece measures 4½ in from beg (do not stretch). Bind off loosely, leaving long end for sewing.

Finishing:

Sew together, stuff and finish as for Father Roly-Poly, making dividing line for body and head just a little above the halfway mark between top and bottom. To make hair, wind the medium brown yarn around the 4¼ in piece of cardboard 16 times. Slip off and tie around the bunch at center with a 10 in length of yarn. Do not cut loops. Sew, arrange, and glue to head as for Father Roly-Poly. Make face in same manner also. Using patterns, cut arms from purple felt, hands from white felt, one large flower for bottom from orange felt and two small flowers from yellow felt—one for collar trim and one to put in hair. Cut a small diamond shape from white felt for center of bottom orange flower and two small circles from orange felt for center of yellow flowers. For collar, measure and cut a ¼ in wide piece of purple felt to fit around neckline. Glue or sew all in place.

Patterns for Roly-Poly Family

Arm (for Father)   Hand (for Father)

(Top)

Arm (for Mother)   Hand (for Mother)

(Top)

Arm (for Baby)   Hand (for Baby)

(Top)

Small flower

Small flower
center

Flower
(for center of
bottom flower
and for
Mother's collar)

Tie

Bottom large flower

Large
flower
center

Sixteen Little Bears

There are bears of all kinds here. There are sitting and standing bears and some I call tall bears (they have longer legs). There are Pandas, Koalas, Polar Bears, Brown Bears, and Black Bears, and each one is wearing a little something special. They range in height from 4¾ inches to 6¾ inches and are all made of knitting worsted weight yarn, by the same general directions except for the different leg lengths and, of course, the use of different yarn color.

It's fun to make them as given, but why not also try changing around the way they're dressed. Use just a ribbon around a Panda's neck, a vest on a Koala, or perhaps a nightgown on a Polar Bear. Try any other trims you may have or can think of for lots and lots of variety.

Some things you'll need to make any of the bears are:

Embroidery floss: Very small amounts of black (for each bear's eyes and nose) OR
Small moving eyes: 2 each for Pandas and Black Bears
Felt: very small amount of black (for Panda's eye patches and Koala's nose)
1 Pair #4 knitting needles
Yarn needle
Sewing thread to match felt, fabric, and trims as given for each bear
Sewing needle
Polyester fiberfill

General directions for knitting and finishing are given here first. Separate directions for each are then given that explain the materials and colors to use and how to dress the bears.

Make a Bear:

Body (make one): Starting at lower edge of body, cast on 20 sts. Work even in St st for 16 rows. (The knit side is the right side.) *Next row* (inc row): *K1, inc 1 st in next st, repeat from * across row—30 sts. Continue for **Head:** Beg with P row, work even in St st for 13 rows. *Next row:* K2 tog across—15 sts. P and bind off. **Arms** (make two) for all Bears and legs (two more) for sitting and standing bears: Starting at upper edge, cast on 10 sts. Work even in St st for 8 rows. **Complete as follows:** Cut yarn, leaving long end for sewing. Thread yarn into yarn needle, and pull through sts as you take them off knitting needle. **Legs For Tall Bears** (make two): Starting at upper edge, cast on 10 sts. Work even in St st for 12 rows. Complete as for arms. **Ears** (make four pieces—two for each ear): Starting at lower edge, cast on 6 sts. Work even in St st for 4 rows.

(The knit side is the right side.) *Next row:* K and dec 1 st each end of row—4 sts. *Next row:* P2 tog twice. Complete as for arms and legs. Sew remaining 2 sts firmly down to top of ear piece, thereby rounding the top of the ear. Run in end on wrong side of piece to hide. **Nose** (make one piece): Cast on 14 sts. Work even in St st for 3 rows. Complete as for arms and legs.

Finishing:

Body and Head: Bring sides of body and head piece together to form a tube (right side out). Using matching yarn, overcast these side edges together. Fold piece flat with seam at center back. Sew piece closed across top of head. Stuff firmly. Sew closed across bottom edge. **To Form Neckline:** Thread a long length of matching yarn into yarn needle. Working on inc row, take a few stitches to secure yarn at back

seam. Wrap yarn around bear twice, pulling hard to pull piece in to form neck. Hold firmly and return to where yarn was secured, and secure again with several stitches **Arms:** Thread yarn that was pulled through last stitches of arm into needle. Pull up tightly, bringing sides together right side out and forming a tube. Fasten securely. Take a few stitches to close lower end completely. Using matching yarn, sew seam where sides were brought together. Stuff firmly. Fold flat across top edge to shut, with seam at one side, and sew closed. Sew onto side of body, facing forward on sitting bear and straight out on standing and tall bears, with seam at underside of arm. **Legs:** Finish all legs and stuff as for arms. **To Sew to Body:** *For sitting bears*—sew onto each side of bear

at lower edge of body, to extend forward same as arms, seam at underside of leg. *For standing bears*—Sew onto lower edge of body to extend down and angled outward a little, seam on inside of leg. *For tall bears*—Sew onto lower edge of body to extend straight down, seam on back or inside of leg. **Ears:** Place two ear pieces together, with right sides out and overcast edges together, working around curved edges twice to make firm. Sew cast-on edges in position at each end of seam on head. **Nose:** Thread yarn that was pulled through last stitches of nose into yarn needle. Pull up tightly to gather, and fasten. Take a few sitches to completely close end of nose. Sew seam formed by pulling sides of piece together. Stuff firmly and sew in place on face, with seam

at underside of nose. **Face:** Using six strands of black embroidery floss, work eyes and tip of nose in satin stitch.

1: BROWN BEAR WITH SCARF

To make this bear you'll need:

Acrylic yarn of knitting worsted weight:
  1 oz brown yarn
  Scraps of dark red, yellow, and orange (for scarf)

Make and finish a tall bear ac-

cording to directions given. Then make a scarf as follows: With dark red, cast on 54 sts. K 1 row. Cut yarn, leaving an end of several inches. Tie on yellow and use to K 2 rows (garter st). Cut yellow, leaving end as before. Tie on orange, K 1 row. *Next row:* K and bind off, leaving end. Thread a few more strands of each color onto each end then gather and tie all strands together near end of scarf to make a tassel effect. Trim ends even. Put around bear's neck and tie at front.

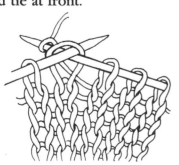

2: GOLDEN BEAR IN GREEN VEST

To make this bear you'll need:

Acrylic yarn of knitting worsted weight: 1 oz gold
Felt: small piece of green (for vest)
Embroidery floss: very small-amount of red and gold

Make and finish a tall bear according to directions. Then make a vest as follows: Using pattern, cut two front pieces and one back piece from green felt. Using matching thread, sew small seams at shoulders and sides. Turn to right side. Using six strands of red

embroidery floss, work Lazy Daisy stitch flowers on each side of front, just above points. Make a few straight stitches at center of flower with two strands of gold floss. Use all six strands of gold floss in needle to lace front together, lacing from bottom to top. Tie in bow at neckline.

3: BROWN BEAR IN RED AND WHITE STRIPED SWEATER

To make this bear you'll need:

Acrylic yarn of knitting worsted
weight:
1 oz brown
½ oz red
A few scraps of white for
sweater.
2 stitch holders.

Make and finish a tall bear according to directions, and then
knit his sweater as follows: Starting at lower front edge with red,
cast on 16 sts. Work in garter st
for 2 rows. Drop red, but do not
cut. Tie on white and use to work
2 rows in garter st. Repeat last 4
rows twice, carrying yarn not in
use up side of work, for a total of
3 red stripes and 3 white stripes.
Cut white. At beg of next 2 rows,
cast on 3 sts for sleeves—22 sts.
Work even in garter st for 6 rows.
Next row: Divide for **Neck:** K6,
put these 6 sts onto a st holder.
Bind off next 10 sts, K to end of
row—6 sts. Work even in garter
st for 5 rows. Cut yarn. Put these
6 sts onto second st holder. Put
sts from first st holder onto right-
hand needle and tie on red yarn
at inside neck edge. Work even
in garter st for 5 rows. *Next row*
Back: K across 6 sts, cast on 10
sts, K6 sts from second st holder—
22 sts. Work even in garter st for
9 rows. At beg of next 2 rows
bind off 3 sts—16 sts. Drop red
(do not cut), tie on white and use
to work 2 rows in garter st. Drop
white, pick up red and use to work
2 rows in garter st. Repeat last
4 rows twice, for a total of 3 white
and 3 red stripes, as on front. Using red, K and bind off. Sew side
and sleeve seam. Put on bear, and
turn back sleeves if you wish.

4–5: BLACK BEARS— BROTHER AND SISTER

To make each bear you'll need:

Acrylic yarn of knitting worsted
weight: 1 oz black
Embroidery floss: small amount
of brown
Plus:
Felt: small piece of yellow
4 very small white buttons (for
brother bear)
8 in of 1½-inch-wide white eyelet trim
15 in of yellow trim (for sister
bear)

Make and finish each according
to directions for a sitting bear, but
sew on small moving eyes instead
of embroidering them, unless the
bear is for a very young child. In
that case, embroidering with
brown floss would be best. Use
brown floss for tip of nose. To
make a vest for the brother bear,
using pattern, cut two front pieces
and one back piece from felt. Using matching thread, sew small
seams at shoulders and sides. Turn
to right side. Sew two buttons on
each side of front opening (but
these, too, should be omitted for
a very young child).

To make a dress for sister bear,
make a narrow hem in one short
end of the eyelet trim and wrap
around waistline for skirt, overlapping raw edge. Cut and wrap
a piece of yellow trim around

waist at top edge of eyelet. Cut
another piece of yellow trim to
fit from right side of front, around
back of neck and back to left side
of front for straps. Sew all in place,
using matching thread and sewing through into bear to hold in
place.

6: KOALA BEAR

To make the koala bear you'll need:

Acrylic yarn of knitting worsted
weight:
1 oz gray
Small amount of tan
12 in of narrow red grosgrain ribbon
Felt: small piece of black

Make and finish a sitting bear
with gray yarn according to directions, with the following exceptions: **Ears:** These are made
a little bit larger and in different
colors. The two pieces for outside of ears are knit using gray
yarn, and the two pieces for inner
ears are knit using the light tan
yarn. **To Make:** Cast on 8 sts. Work
even in St st for 5 rows. *Next
row:* P and dec 1 st each end of
row—6 sts. *Next row:* K and dec
1 st each end of row—4 sts. *Next
row:* P2 tog twice. Complete as
for all ears. Place one gray piece
(outside) and one light tan piece
(inside) together with right sides
(knit sides) out, and, using gray
yarn, sew together, taking large

stitches around curved edges. Sew cast-on edges to head, with ears extending straight out from sides of head. **Nose:** This is made a bit smaller and with gray yarn. **To Make:** Cast on 14 sts. Work even in St st for 2 rows. Complete, finish, and sew in place as for all others. Using pattern, cut a nose patch from black felt and, using matching thread, sew in place on nose. Make eyes the same with black floss. Place ribbon around neck and tie in bow.

7: PANDA WITH RED BANDANA

To make this panda bear, you'll need:

Acrylic yarn of knitting worsted weight:
½ oz black
½ oz white
Small piece of red bandana fabric
Felt: Small piece of black
2 small moving eyes

Follow general directions for knitting and finishing a tall bear, using white yarn for body and head piece and the nose, and black yarn for arms, legs, and ears. Using pattern, cut two eye patches from black felt and sew in place with matching thread. Sew moving eyes in place on top of patches (or else cut top part of eyes from white felt, or embroider them). Embroider tip of nose with black

floss. Using pattern, cut out red bandana. Make a narrow hem around all edges. Place around neck and tie at back, allowing to hang down in point at front.

8: PANDA WITH SAILOR COLLAR

To make this panda bear you'll need:

Acrylic yarn of knitted worsted weight:
½ oz black
½ oz white
Small piece of blue and white striped fabric
12 in of narrow red rick-rack
Felt: small pieces of blue and black
2 small moving eyes

Make and finish a sitting bear, using white for body and head piece and nose, and black for arms, legs, and ears. Using pattern, cut two eye patches from black felt and sew in place with matching thread. Sew moving eyes in place on top of patches or finish making them from felt or embroidery. Embroider tip of nose with black floss. Using patterns, cut collar from blue felt and insert from striped fabric. Hem all sides of striped fabric, and sew in place right onto front of bear's chest. Sew rick-rack in place around outer edge of collar, allowing ends to hang down an inch or so below points of collar. Place collar

around neck covering edges of insert and sew firmly at point to front of bear to hold in place.

9: GOLDEN BEAR WITH FLOWER CHAIN

To make this bear you'll need:

Acrylic yarn of knitted worsted weight:
1 oz gold
Small amounts of many different colors (for flowers)

Make and finish a sitting bear according to directions. To make a "flower": Take a piece of any color yarn, long enough to wind around your finger four times. Cut end and slip off carefully into a bundle. Hold firmly together and tie all together around middle of bundle with a short length of yellow (or whatever color you wish) yarn. Cut ends even. Make enough "flowers" of different colors—or all one color, if you prefer—to fit around neck of bear. Measure a length of green yarn (or any color) long enough to fit around bear's neck, plus enough for tying, and thread into yarn needle. Thread all the "flowers" onto this yarn, put onto bear around neck, tie and trim ends.

10: POLAR BEAR

To make this polar bear you'll need:

Acrylic yarn of knitting worsted
   weight:
   1 oz white (for bear's body)
   ½ oz blue
   Few yd green (for sweater and
     cap)
Stitch holder

Make and finish a tall bear according to directions, then dress him in his sweater and cap made by the following directions: **Sweater:** Beg at lower back edge, with green, cast on 16 sts. Cut green, tie on blue and work ribbing of K1, P1 for 6 rows. At the beg of next 2 rows, cast on 4 sts for sleeves—24 sts. Work even in ribbing as established for 6 rows. *Next row:* Work across 6 sts, place these 6 sts onto a st holder, bind off next 12 sts (for back of neck), and work across last 6 sts. **First Side:** Working on 6 sts of one side only, work in ribbing for 3 rows. At beg of next row, cast on 6 sts for front. Work even in ribbing for 4 rows. At beg of next row, bind off 4 sts of sleeve. Work even on 8 sts for 6 rows. Cut blue, tie on green and work 1 row. Bind off loosely in ribbing, with green. **Second Side:** Place sts from holder onto needle with point toward neck edge. Tie on blue yarn, turn work, and work in ribbing for 4 rows. At beg of next row, cast on 6 sts for front. Work even in ribbing for 4 more

rows. At beg of next row, bind off 4 sts of sleeve. Work even on 8 sts for 6 rows. Cut blue, tie on green and work 1 row. Bind off loosely in ribbing with green. Sew underarm and side seams with matching yarn and overcast st. **Neck Ribbing:** Using green, with right side facing, pick up and knit 28 sts around neck edge. Work 1 row in ribbing. Cut green, tie on blue and work 1 row in ribbing. Bind off loosely in ribbing with blue. Hide yarn ends in work. Put sweater on bear and sew front together up to neck ribbing, using matching yarn and overcast stitch. **Cap:** Using green, cast on 28 sts. Work in ribbing of K1, P1 for 1 row. Cut green, tie on blue and work in St st for 2 rows (the knit side is right side). *Next row:* *K2, K2 tog, repeat from * across row—21 sts. P 1 row. *Next row:* *K1, K2 tog, repeat from * across row—14 sts. P 1 row. *Next row:* K2 tog across—7 sts. *Next row:* P2 tog across to last st, end P1—4 sts. Cut yarn, leaving end for sewing. Thread yarn into needle, and pull through sts as you take them off knitting needle. Sew seam. To make a pom-pom of green yarn, wind yarn around finger 15 times. Slip off carefully and tie bundle tightly together around center. Cut all loops. Fluff up and trim evenly. Sew to top of cap. With green yarn, sew cap to bear's head, placing over one ear.

11: BROWN BEAR WITH BIKINI

To make this bear you'll need:

Acrylic yarn of knitting worsted
   weight:
   1 oz brown
   Very small amount of red
Red polka-dot fabric:
   2 pieces 3¼ × 3¾ in (for bottom)
   1 piece 1½ × 5¾ in (for top)
1 large darning needle

Make and finish a standing bear according to directions. **To Make Bikini Bottom:** Hold the two pieces of fabric for bottom tog, wrong sides out. Making a very narrow seam, sew tog around 3 sides. Turn right side out, fold in raw edges on fourth side, and slip st closed. Place on bear, diaper fashion. Thread a length of red yarn into darning needle and pull this through top edges of bikini bottom at right side. Remove needle and tie yarn ends in bow on side. Repeat for left side. Trim ends. **To Make Top:** Fold top piece lengthwise wrong side out. Sew long side and one end with narrow seam. Turn right side out. Close end as for bottom. Place around bear with ends meeting at center back. Tie with red yarn as for bottom. To make a tie to go around the neck, cut a length of yarn, tie the middle of it around the center front of bikini top, pull ends up and around to back of neck and tie in bow there.

12: SANTA BEAR

To make this bear you'll need:

Acrylic yarn of knitting worsted
    weight: 1 oz dark brown
8½ in white bias tape
Felt: 6 × 9 in piece of red
2 white pom-poms
Fabric glue

Make and finish a standing bear according to directions. Using patterns, cut out one shirt piece and two hat pieces (two alike) from red felt. Cut along dotted line on front of shirt to open from neck to bottom. Fold piece over in half at shoulders and sew a narrow seam at each underarm and side of shirt. Put on bear, overlapping front opening a little. Cut a piece of bias tape and place flat on front over the opening overlap. Using matching thread, sew in place while on bear. Cut a piece of bias tape to fit around lower edge of shirt and sew in place as for front strip. Making a very narrow seam along the two long sides of hat pieces, sew them together. Turn right side out. Put onto bear's head, placing over one ear. Fold tip end down to front and hold in place with a few stitches. Glue one white pom-pom to tip end of hat and one to front of shirt under chin.

13: CLOWN BEAR

To make this bear you'll need:

Acrylic yarn of knitting worsted
    weight: 1 oz beige
Felt:
    4 × 8½ in piece of purple
    4 × 8½ in piece of fuchsia
8 pom-poms in assorted colors
    (whatever you like)
Fabric glue

Make and finish a standing bear according to directions, and dress him up as a clown. To make neck ruffle, cut a strip of purple felt 1 by 8½ in. Cut a strip of fuchsia felt ¾ by 8½ in. Place the fuchsia felt piece on top of the purple piece and, with matching thread, gather one long edge to fit around bear's neck. Put ruffle around neck, ends meeting at back, and sew in place. Using pattern for hat, cut two pieces from purple felt and two pieces from fuchsia felt. Place all four pieces together with two purple pieces on inside and two fuchsia pieces on outside. Sew all together with a very narrow seam along the two long sides. Turn right-side-out (purple is now on the outside). Turn up about ½ in at bottom edge for a brim on hat (fuchsia is on outside of brim). Place on bear's head—over one ear—and take a few stitches to secure. Glue two pom-poms (any color) onto front of hat. Glue five pom-poms on top of ruffle along front of neck, and glue one to front of bear just below collar.

14–15: BEDTIME BEARS—BOY AND GIRL

To make the Bedtime Bears you'll need:

Acrylic yarn of knitting worsted
    weight: 1 oz dark brown for
    each
Plus:
⅛ yd red-and-white striped flan-
    nel fabric
2 very small white buttons
    (for the boy bear)

Small amount of red yarn (for boy
    bear)
⅛ yd small print flannel fabric (I've
    used an aqua-and-yellow
    print)
18 in narrow yellow ribbon
    (for the girl bear)

Make and finish each one according to directions for a tall bear. **Make Night shirt for boy Bedtime Bear:** Using patterns, cut out one back piece and two front pieces from flannel. Making very narrow seams with right sides together, sew together at shoulders. Make a small hem on sleeve edges, then sew underarm and side seams. Make a narrow hem both at neckline and bottom edge of night shirt. Turn right side out. Place on bear, overlapping fronts to close and sew one front down to second front. Sew the buttons on front just below neckline, placing one above the other. **Nightcap:** Using pattern, cut out two pieces from flannel. With right sides tog, sew a narrow seam along each of the two long sides. Make a narrow hem along bottom edge. Turn right side out. Make a large tassel from red yarn and sew to tip of cap. Place night cap on bear's head, over one ear and sew in place.

Make Nightgown for girl Bedtime Bear: Using patterns, cut out, sew together and put on bear just as for the boy's nightshirt. Sew the front together as before, but instead of adding the buttons, make a small bow of ribbon and sew in place on front, just below neckline.

Nightcap: Using patterns, cut out two large circles and one small circle from flannel. Holding the two large circles together, wrong sides out, stitch together with a ¼ in seam around outside, leaving 1 in or so open for turning. Turn right side out. Slip stitch opening closed. Run a gathering thread around flannel circle ½ in inside of edge. Pull up to make a small cap with crown opening about 1¼ in across. Fasten and sew around gathering line again to hold cap in shape. Using enough polyester fiberfill stuffing to fill the crown of the cap, wrap this ball of stuffing in the smaller circle of flannel and put into crown of cap with the raw edges inside, out of sight. Place cap on bear's head between ears and sew in place all around crown. Put a piece of ribbon around crown and tie in bow at front. Take a few stitches with matching thread to hold ribbon in place.

16: SWEETHEART BEAR

For this bear you'll need:

Acrylic yarn of knitting worsted weight: 1 oz of beige

14 in of narrow striped ribbon
Felt: very small piece of red

Make and finish a standing bear according to directions, then dress him up in a little harness with a big heart on it, as follows: **Harness:** Measure and cut a piece of ribbon to fit around middle of bear. Measure and cut a piece of ribbon for each shoulder strap, long enough to go from front waistline piece, over shoulders, cross in back and go down to back waistline piece. Sew all in place on bear, sewing through to bear in a few places to secure. Using pattern, cut a heart from red felt. With matching thread, sew in place on front of harness, attaching point of heart to waistline ribbon piece and side edges of heart to sides of shoulder straps.

Patterns for Sixteen Little Bears

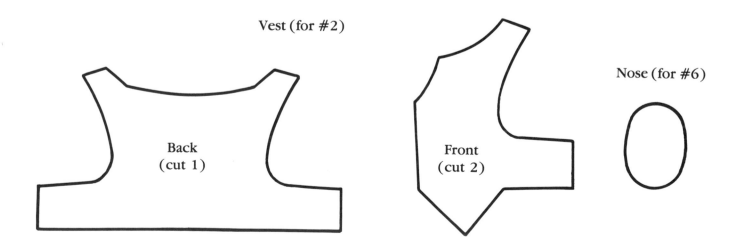

Vest (for #2)

Back
(cut 1)

Front
(cut 2)

Nose (for #6)

Vest (for #4)

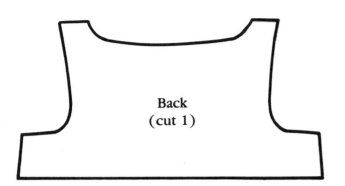

Back
(cut 1)

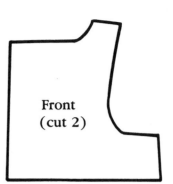

Front
(cut 2)

Eye (for #7 and #8)

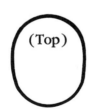

(Top)

Heart
(for #16)

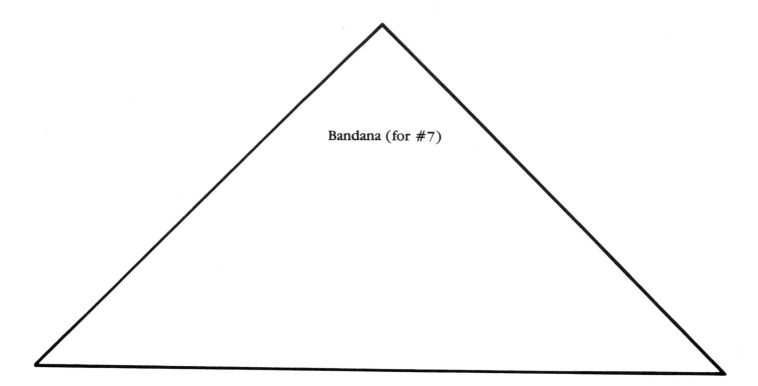

Bandana (for #7)

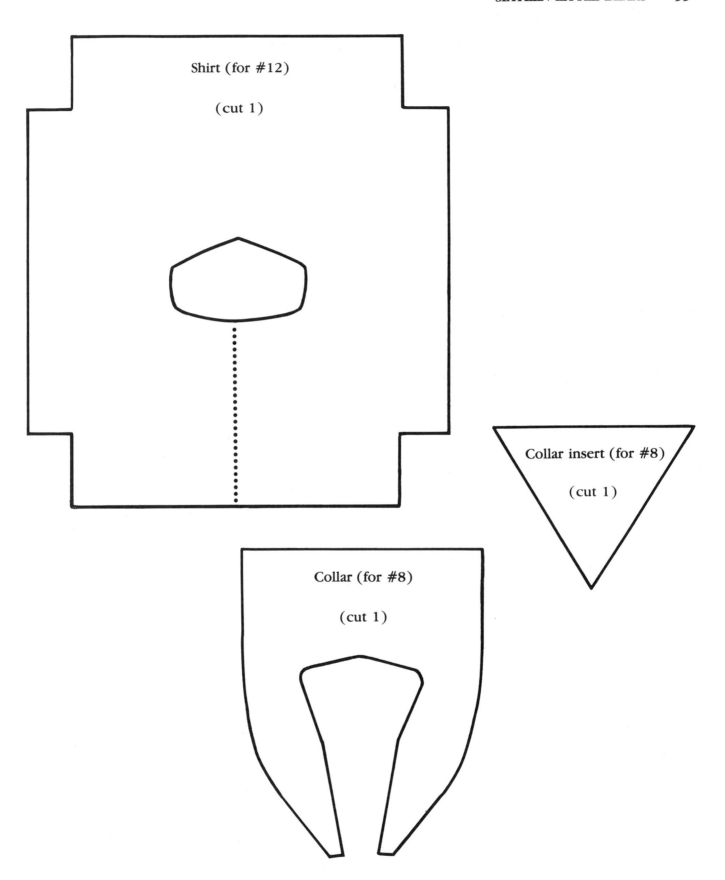

Shirt (for #12)

(cut 1)

Collar insert (for #8)

(cut 1)

Collar (for #8)

(cut 1)

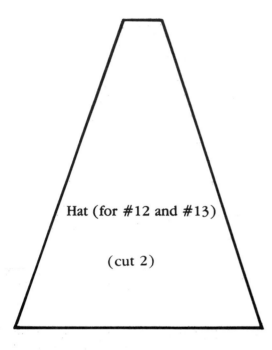

Hat (for #12 and #13)

(cut 2)

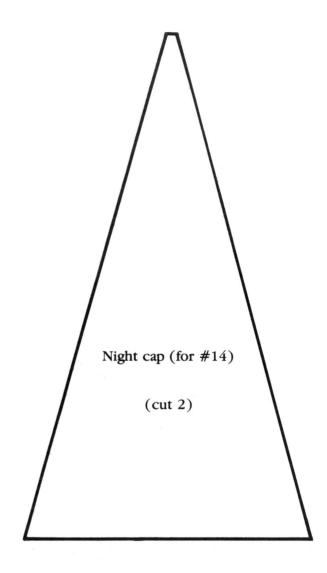

Night cap (for #14)

(cut 2)

Nightgown (for #14 and #15)

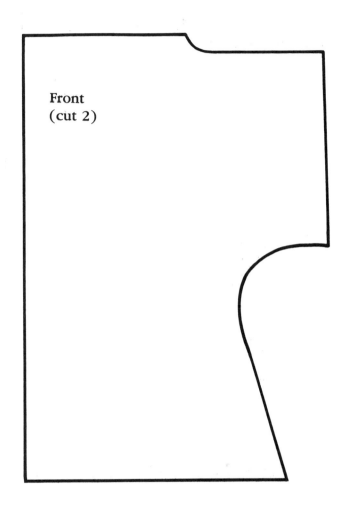

Front
(cut 2)

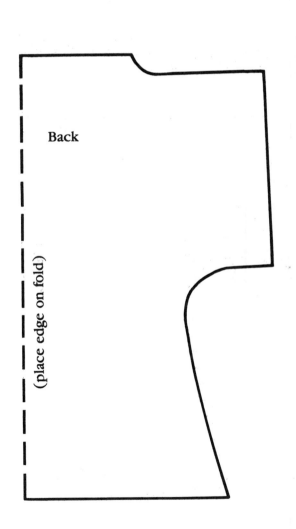

Back

(place edge on fold)

Night cap (for #15)

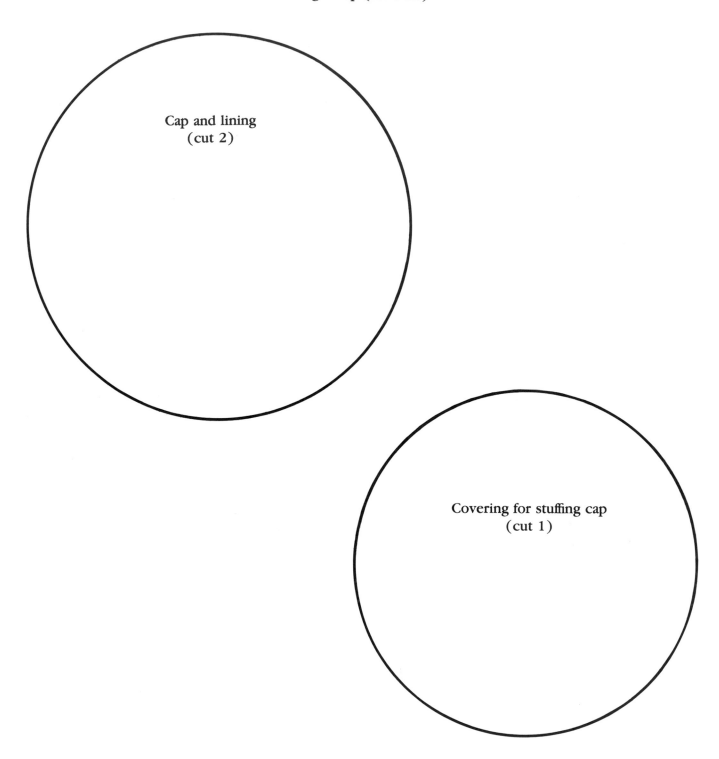

Cap and lining
(cut 2)

Covering for stuffing cap
(cut 1)